**What F**

**Rober**

"Rob's belief in my potential has been a driving force in my growth. His encouragement has helped me push beyond my limitations and reach for goals in areas where I was losing hope. Rob excels not only as a business leader but also as a role model for husbands and fathers. His dedication to family and consistent demonstration of values create a loving, supportive environment for those around him. Rob's genuine care for others makes him a true gem. His remarkable patience and ability to remain calm in the face of challenges are testaments to his inner strength. My only regret is not knowing Rob sooner. His positive influence has been profound, and I can only imagine the impact he could have had if our paths had crossed earlier. I am honored to call him my friend and mentor."

— Dennis Isip, Real Estate Agent

"I am so grateful for Robert coming into our daughter's life at just the right time. He helped her find the strength she already had inside her, just as he does with everyone he touches."

— Jeri Bellona, Mother-in-Law

"As my peer in the real estate industry, Rob's tireless efforts on behalf of those he loves restored my faith in sales and has had a profound impact on my life. When I decided to pivot my real estate career from residential to right of way, Rob was the first person I called. Through Rob's steadfast guidance, I was able to find the honor and integrity in my career that I so desperately craved. I'll never be able to repay him for everything he's done for me. I'm sure his response to that would be, 'Just take care of someone else today.' Now he's finally written a book, and I am so thrilled for all of you who now get to meet Rob and hear his story."

— Tina Thorson, Friend and Author of *Breathe It Out: Conquering the Nine Fears That Are Holding You Back*

"Robert Henry is the epitome of integrity and self-respect. He sets high standards and boundaries, and he doesn't just talk the talk; he walks it with unwavering commitment. Many might perceive Robert as having it all, and in many ways, they're right. He doesn't rely on external validation to define his worth. Instead, he passionately upholds his principles and lives by them every day. His dedication to his values is not just commendable; it's truly inspirational."

— Geoffrey VanDenKooy, Friend and Business Owner

"I was shocked when I learned about Rob's past. I had assumed he had enjoyed a privileged childhood, given his personal and professional success. His incredible story is heart-wrenching, yet he chose to transform his experiences into a journey of self-acceptance and renewal. Rob's inspiring words offer hope to all who seek to overcome pain and regret and to build a happy life."

— Tracie Riekena, Friend

"It requires immense courage to build the life of your dreams, even more so when life is challenging. What inspires me greatly about Rob is his readiness to invest in his vision and his people, particularly in the beginning, before the momentum of success began to build. Rob possesses a unique balance of humility and conviction. He is open to learning rather than pretending to know it all. He is also ready to challenge you and encourage you to aim higher. Surrounding yourself with individuals who are fully committed to their vision is powerful. That is why I am honored to call Rob a friend."

— Chris Angell, Friend and Author of
*The Freedom Challenge*

"Rob possesses a profound desire to guide people and is an inherent teacher. You can consistently rely on him to provide guidance with his extensive knowledge and life experience. He never settles for what he already knows; instead, he thrives on growth, continually pushing himself to learn and develop. Rob is passionate about personal development and excels at helping others become their best selves."

— Chris Perry, Friend

"Getting to know Robert has taught me that despite all the foolish actions I've taken and mistakes I've made in my life, I can still attain greatness. Robert is a genuine champion."

— Kevin Johnson, Business Owner

"I first met Rob many years ago when he participated in a leadership training program I had the honor of leading. Since then, I have followed his journey into real estate and have observed him swiftly become a master in the field. What stands out most about Rob is his unwavering commitment to empowering others and bringing out their best qualities. I know few people who do it as well as he does. In many ways, the student has become the teacher. I am constantly inspired to broaden my horizons and challenge my own limits as I observe Rob in action. I frequently adopt his ideas, and I consider myself fortunate to have gotten to know him as well as I have."

— Aaron Hendon, Managing Broker,
Author, Speaker, Mentor, and Friend

"Robert Henry serves as a powerful testament to resilience. Faced with challenging circumstances and hitting rock bottom in prison, he turned inward and made the conscious decision to change his trajectory. Upon his release, his true journey commenced. He underscores the significance of learning, emphasizing both the method and the mentors. His success stands as a testament to unwavering resilience, reminding us that life may knock us down more often than it lifts us up. However, with focused determination, a willingness to learn, and a genuine heart, we can all find our way and persevere on our unique paths. Thank you, Robert, for everything you have taught, for your continuous pursuit of knowledge, and for the positive impact you have on so many lives."

— Darin Watkins, Friend, Mentor, and Author of
*Chance for Glory: The Innovation and Triumph of the Washington State 1916 Rose Bowl Team*

"Robert has been a teacher since our first meeting, and this role is at the core of his identity. I often jest that each time we meet, I invariably learn something new. His life experiences have cultivated his generous spirit, and his readiness to share lessons from his failures, redemption, and successes is truly remarkable."

— Mike Ferguson, Marketing Professional

"To merely state that Robert Henry has made significant contributions to my life would be a gross understatement. I can assert with certainty that my life has been enriched through meeting, being mentored by, and following Rob's leadership. When he advises action, I take it. As a result, I am now living life on my own terms, according to my own schedule. I have earned 30k in commissions while on vacation, all without missing a single precious moment with my family. I feel incredibly blessed and grateful to have chosen to follow such a passionate, caring, and straightforward mentor."

— Hannah Masters, Real Estate Agent

"In *Unleashing Your Own Potential*, Robert Henry, a former bank robber, teaches us to look closely at the decisions we make and make better ones. He knows from experience how important it is to make the right kinds of decisions because they can determine our destiny. He changed his world by choosing not to run from the law any longer and to improve his life in healthy ways. His successful career in real estate and the personal happiness he's found are testaments that the right decision can open doors to achieving your full potential."

— Patrick Snow. Coach, Mentor, and International Bestselling Author of *Creating Your Own Destiny* and *The Affluent Entrepreneur*

"In *Unleashing Your Own Potential*, Robert Henry shares his incredible story that amplifies the truth that we always have a choice. No matter our circumstances, Robert reveals that when we make the right decisions, we can change our world and achieve lasting success, happiness, and personal fulfillment. You'll feel like you've robbed the bank with all the riches you'll get from this book."

— Nicole Gabriel, Author of *Finding Your Inner Truth*
and *Stepping Into Your Becoming*

"Rarely have I read as compelling a story as Robert Henry's, and best of all, he uses that story to analyze the mistakes he made and highlight what he changed to make things right. *Unleashing Your Own Potential* is one of the rare personal development books you'll not only never forget, but want to read again and again."

— Tyler R. Tichelaar, PhD and Award-Winning Author of
*Narrow Lives* and *The Best Place*

YOUR SETBACK IS A SETUP FOR YOUR COMEBACK

# UNLEASHING YOUR OWN POTENTIAL

THE SELF-LEADERSHIP JOURNEY
FROM ROCK BOTTOM TO PROSPERITY (AND BEYOND)

ROBERT W. HENRY

PUBLISHING
New York

**UNLEASHING YOUR OWN POTENTIAL:**
**The Self-Leadership Journey from Rock Bottom to Prosperity (and Beyond)**



Published by:
Aviva Publishing
Lake Placid, NY
(518) 523-1320
www.AvivaPubs.com



Address all inquiries to:
Robert Henry
304 W Pacific Ave, Ste 310
Spokane, WA 99201
(509) 413-9634
Robert@HavenRealEstateGroup.com
www.UnleashingYourOwnPotential.com

ISBN: 978-1-63618-311-4
Library of Congress Control Number: 2023919514
Editing: Superior Book Productions
Cover Design and Interior Book Layout: Nicole Gabriel, Angel Dog Productions
Author Photo: Rachel French

Every attempt has been made to properly source all quotes.

Printed in the United States of America

First Edition

2 4 6 8 10 12

# DEDICATION

*To Cambria, My Wife and Guiding Light,*

In the storms of life, you are the lighthouse that guides me to safety. You're the strong anchor that holds me steady, allowing me to navigate the most unpredictable waters. Your ceaseless belief in me has been my source of courage to dig deep, revealing both my vulnerabilities and strengths in this book. You are not just someone I lean on; you're the essence of everything good in me. Thank you for always being my North Star, a constant beacon that leads me out of darkness and into a world bright with possibilities.

*To My Extraordinary Daughters, Kiaya, Olivia, and Mady,*

Each of you is a heartbeat that gives rhythm to my life's song. Your laughter is my music, your dreams my guiding horizon, and your love is the sustenance for all my hopes. I wrote this book with your faces in my mind and your future in my heart. I hope as you leaf through these pages, you see them not just as words, but as signposts on the journey of life.

My aspiration is for you to see setbacks not as roadblocks but as steppingstones—ones that help you build a pathway to the life you envision. As you grow, I hope you'll pass this outlook on to your own children, creating a legacy of strong, self-empowered women who seize life unapologetically. With every lesson I've learned and every page I've written, your smiles fueled my soul. You are my ultimate motivation and my most cherished reward.

*To the Exceptional Employees and Agents of the Haven Family,*

Your trust in Cambria and me for your career growth is an honor I deeply cherish. Your dedication not only builds our company but constantly inspires my growth. May this book shed light on the experiences that fuel my passion to lead you all to success.

*To You, My Valued Reader,*

Sharing my life story and the lessons I learned with you is both an honor and a responsibility I don't take lightly. Writing this book was an emotional balancing act—on one side, the weight of the shame attached to my past mistakes and traumas, and on the other, an intense obligation to provide an unfiltered, genuine narrative. I peeled back the layers of my life, exposing moments I am not proud of, but I did so to show you the transformation possible when you dare to confront your flaws and limitations head-on.

Through speaking engagements, from classrooms to corporate events and even informal chats around campfires, I have discovered when one person opens up about their journey, it gives others the courage to examine their own. I sincerely hope this book serves as a tool to help you navigate your own setbacks, inspiring you to take the reins of your life.

Thank you for giving me the opportunity to be part of your life's journey, even if just through these pages.

Your time is a gift, and the honor of being a guide in your life is one I cherish deeply.

With profound and heartfelt gratitude,

Robert W. Henry

# ACKNOWLEDGMENTS

Cambria Henry, Kiaya Henry, Olivia Henry, Madison Moore, Morgan and Christa Henry, Donald Smith, John and Jeri Belona, Karen Schubert, Raschell Savage, Taylor Henry, Jake Savage, Andy and Beverly Schubert, Chris and Kahla Perry, Aaron Scott and Stephanie Hunter, Amber Scott, Patricia Honea, Ginger Lewallen, Rod and Donna Boast, Geoff and Kim Van Den Kooy, Chris and Jenny Angell, Jan and Jo McHenry, Tony and Sage Robbins, Jon Cheplak, Bill Pipes, Wayne Salmans, Steve and Laurie Garcia, Emily Faylor, Aaron Hendon, Alex Aanderud, Alvera Gaskins, Jessica White, Shane Workman, Dale and Jessica Cargile, Greg Grmolyes, Jennifer Tiffany, Colleen Streeter, Michael and Christy Green, Gary and Traci Riekena, Alen and Amber Pinkerton, Richard and Brandy Fries, Dave and Karen Merritt, Dave and Christi Pittiglio, Mike and Kim Dawson, Jordan and Haley Rippee, Brent and Katie Huckabee, Marv and Kathy Mathis, and all who have graciously and generously contributed to my growth, and ultimately, a splendid life.

# UNLEASHING YOUR OWN POTENTIAL

with Robert Henry

# CONTENTS

1 The Power of Decision-Making: How to Optimize Your Choices for a Better Life

2 Defining Your Own Destiny: Thriving Despite Adversity

3 Taking Charge of Your Life: How to Break Free from the Grip of Circumstances

4 Forgetting Your Values: The Slippery Slope of Compromising Your Integrity

5 Facing the Consequences: Taking Ownership of Your Decisions

6 Setting a Personal Standard: How to Unleash Your Potential

7 Choosing to Thrive: The Power of Daily Rituals and Focusing on the Present

8 The Science of Gratitude: How Positive Emotions Boost Success and Well-Being

9 Building a Support System: The Role of Relationships in Personal Growth and Success

10 Overcoming Adversity: All Journeys Will Entail Setbacks

11 Self-Leadership: Charting Your Personal Path to Success

12 Embracing a Beginner's Mind: The Power of Curiosity and Continuous Learning

Recommended Reading

About the Author

Book Robert Henry to Speak at Your Next Event

Robert Henry Coaching

# UNLEASHING YOUR OWN POTENTIAL

with Robert Henry

# 1

# THE POWER OF DECISION-MAKING: HOW TO OPTIMIZE YOUR CHOICES FOR A BETTER LIFE

*"You are not stuck where you are unless you decide to be."*

— Dr. Wayne Dyer

Trapped behind bars, with the harsh reality of perhaps a life sentence, I came to a fork in the road. As the weight of my crimes and the overwhelming despair of prison life set in, an opportunity presented itself—the chance to escape. With only two weeks of experience navigating the treacherous halls of a maximum-security prison, I was faced with a decision that would alter the course of my life forever.

The sound of clanging metal bars and echoing footsteps filled the sterile prison hallway as I stood there with adrenaline pumping through my veins. I was nervously waiting for the corrections officer assigned to escort me, who had disappeared into the office of a prison administrator's assistant for a flirtatious chat. The frigid air couldn't cool the beads of sweat forming on my forehead as I waited in anticipation. In this seemingly ordinary moment, surrounded by the prison's harsh reality, I sensed this would prove to be a defining moment in my journey.

The corrections officer had taken me into the basement of the Federal Metropolitan Correctional Institution in downtown San Diego, where the FBI had booked me only two weeks before. The familiar sally port loomed ahead, a secure access point for vehicles, staff, and prisoners. Its reinforced steel door and armed guards were a testament to its purpose: to prevent unauthorized entry or escape. But this time, the steel door was wide open, and the garage door the FBI agents had once walked me through was open, offering a tantalizing glimpse of the "real" world outside.

My heart and thoughts raced as I gazed beyond the garage door entry to the bustling streets of downtown San Diego. A sloped driveway and a stack of pallets offered a tantalizing escape route, leading to an outdoor mall teeming with people. I stood dressed in stark contrast to the typical prisoner garb—a simple white T-shirt, khaki pants, and canvas slip-on shoes. The Federal inmate uniform is far from what you see on TV, and I didn't fit the mold of a federal inmate, nor did I embody the stereotypical prisoner.

At twenty-six, I found myself at a crossroads that would change my life forever. Indicted for bank robbery, I knew the harsh reality of the federal sentencing guideline of twenty years was upon me. But the FBI wasn't satisfied with just one crime because they suspected me of a string of heists. Their hunch was correct. Over the previous eighteen months, I had pulled off ten bank robberies in two states. With the pressure mounting and the fear of facing twenty years for each crime, I was at a crucial turning point. Should I confess everything in the hopes of leniency, or should I take a risk and try to make a break for it? The choice was mine, and my future hung in the balance.

The thought of everything I would have to do to escape successfully was daunting. If caught by the US Marshals, which seemed inevitable given their relentless pursuit of criminals like me, it would surely be game over.

I thought about all the things I would need to do. Change out of my prison uniform into something less identifiable by pursuing authorities so no one could recognize me as an escaped convict, hotwire a nearby car, and speed away before anyone knew what hit them, or more likely, car-jack some poor, unsuspecting person because I don't know how to hot-wire a car. This would leave someone on the side of the road to draw attention, all while I was trying to avoid getting spotted by any guards or officers who were always on high alert within this highly restricted area.

My pulse raced as adrenaline surged through me while I imagined making it beyond the perimeter unseen and speeding away from the prison grounds with reckless abandon. If I got far enough away not to be heard or seen by anyone at the prison gates, I would immediately tense up again as reality hit me like a ton of bricks: I would be on the run from law enforcement officers who held all the cards—namely helicopters equipped with thermal cameras—I had no chance of getting away unless pure luck smiled upon me.

To get to Mexico City, I'd have to spend hours driving non-stop along back roads and hidden highways, with only short stops here and there for bathroom breaks or quick meals. I'd have to steal food from convenience stores that were either unattended or easy enough to rob without too much risk.

Once in Mexico, I'd settle down in a dodgy motel located well out of town where no questions were asked nor identification papers required for check-in. The motel would function as both a safe house and hideout from authorities who would be looking for me relentlessly throughout Mexico City, where I'd surely stand out like a sore thumb.

But then, suddenly, a deep sense of calm overtook me as I remembered a decision I had made just days after my arrest. That decision had the power to shape my entire future. My choice would determine whether I chose to be on the run the rest of my life or I stayed put.

What was this life-altering decision? What brought such a sense of peace and certainty to that intense uncertainty? The decision would ultimately determine my fate and shape the rest of my life. Standing there, I couldn't help wondering how my decision would completely change my future. Would I be able to live with the consequences? Only time would tell.

## How Your Brain Is Wired to Make Decisions

Every day, we make thousands of decisions—some trivial and some with life-changing implications. However, many of these decisions happen subconsciously, without us even being aware of them. Research shows that up to 95 percent of our decision-making occurs in the subconscious mind.

Understanding how the brain works concerning decision-making is essential to improving our choices. Experts in cognitive neuroscience, such as Mark Bowden, Richard Passingham, David Eagleman, Daniel Kahneman, and Dan Heath, have all shed light on this fascinating topic.

The brain has evolved to make decisions based on survival, and as such, we are hardwired to favor immediate rewards over long-term gains. Kahneman calls this the "fast" or "intuitive" decision-making system. It's the part of our brain designed to help us make quick, efficient decisions in the face of danger or other stimuli.

On the other hand, we have the "slow" or "rational" system, which is responsible for more deliberate decision-making. This part of our brain allows us to weigh the pros and cons of a situation and make decisions based on long-term outcomes.

Unfortunately, our fast system dominates our decision-making, even when it's not in our best interest. This domination can lead to impulsive decisions that don't align with our long-term goals.

To make better decisions, we must train ourselves to engage our rational system more often. That means slowing down and being more intentional about our choices. By taking the time to evaluate our options and consider our decisions' potential consequences, we can make more informed choices that are more likely to lead to our desired outcomes.

In addition, it's essential to be aware of our cognitive biases, which can cloud our judgment and lead us to make decisions not in our best interest. By being aware of these biases, we can work to counteract them and make more rational decisions.

Setting clear goals and priorities is another critical factor in optimizing our choices. When we have a clear sense of what we want to achieve, we are more likely to make decisions aligned with those goals. Having goals can help us avoid getting sidetracked by short-term rewards that don't align with our larger aspirations.

Cultivating a growth mindset is crucial to making optimal decisions. With a growth mindset, we believe we can improve our abilities and qualities through effort and education. With a growth mindset, we are more likely to take risks and make decisions that challenge us, even if they are outside of our comfort zone. These experiences can help us learn and grow, leading to more opportunities and a greater sense of fulfillment.

Conditioning is teaching or training a person to behave or respond in a particular way. Our brain is malleable and can be trained to make better decisions, just like it can be trained at any other skill. We must first understand our values, goals, and objectives to condition ourselves. Our choices should align with our core values and help us achieve our goals. Once we have clarity about our values and goals, we can evaluate our options based on how they align with these principles.

Becoming comfortable with uncertainty is another way to optimize our decision-making. Uncertainty is a natural part of the decision-making process and can be intimidating. But we must learn to embrace it and use it to our advantage. This process requires taking the time to gather information and thoroughly evaluate all options before making a decision. Don't be afraid to ask questions, seek advice from others, and challenge assumptions. By doing so, you can reduce uncertainty and make more informed decisions.

Practicing mindful thinking is another critical technique to improve decision-making skills. Mindfulness is being present and fully engaged in the moment without judgment. Conscious thought helps you slow down and focus on what is essential so you can make better decisions. Mindfulness can help you recognize when you are making a decision based on emotions rather than logic or reason. It can also help you notice any biases or assumptions and enable you to evaluate them more objectively. By being more mindful and self-aware, you can improve your decision-making by avoiding impulsive choices that don't align with your long-term goals.

Being open to feedback is another essential factor in optimizing your decision-making. Feedback is critical for growth and can help you recognize your strengths and weaknesses. It's important to seek feedback from others, especially those who may have a different perspective or experience. Feedback can help you evaluate your decisions more objectively and make more informed choices in the future.

For instance, let's say you're trying to decide whether to leave your current job to start a new business. Seeking feedback from people who have started their own businesses can provide valuable insights into the challenges and rewards of entrepreneurship. While feedback is not the only factor to consider when making a decision, it can help you broaden your perspective and identify potential blind spots.

Finally, taking action and following through with your decisions is crucial. Even the best decision is meaningless if you don't follow through. Once you have made a choice, take action and commit to it. Don't let fear or uncertainty hold you back. Instead, focus on your values, goals, and objectives, and act to achieve them.

For example, let's say you've decided to start a new fitness routine to improve your health. To follow through with your decision, you could join a gym, hire a personal trainer, or find an accountability partner to help you stay on track. You'll be more likely to achieve your desired outcome by committing to your decision and taking action.

The power of decision-making is immense; it is an essential skill for success in all areas of life. Our brain makes thousands of decisions every day, and it's critical to be aware of the decision-making process so we can optimize it for better outcomes. By conditioning ourselves, becoming comfortable with uncertainty, practicing mindful thinking, being open to feedback, and acting, we can improve our decision-making skills and create a better life. Remember, every decision can shape our lives, so let's choose wisely.

Here are some daily practices or activities that can help improve your decision-making capabilities over time:

- **Meditate:** Meditation is a great way to clear your mind and focus on the present moment. Regular meditation can improve your decision-making ability by reducing stress, improving focus, and helping you think more clearly.

- **Get enough sleep:** Lack of sleep can negatively affect your decision-making capabilities. Make sure you get enough sleep every night to give your brain the rest it needs to function optimally.

- **Exercise:** Exercise can help reduce stress, clear your mind, and improve your overall mood. You'll then have a more positive outlook and more focus.

- **Read:** Reading can expand your knowledge and help you see different perspectives on various topics.

- **Journal:** Writing down your thoughts, goals, and ideas can help you clarify your thinking and develop a better understanding of your thought processes.

- **Seek feedback:** Getting feedback from those you trust can help you see things from a different perspective and gain new insights.

- **Make lists:** Lists can help you organize your thoughts and prioritize your tasks. Making a pros and cons list will give you a clearer understanding of your options and the consequences of your choices.

- **Practice mindfulness:** Mindfulness involves being fully present in the moment, without judgment. It allows you to stay focused on the present and not be distracted by past experiences or worries about the future. Mindfulness helps to bring clarity and calm to your mind, allowing you to make better decisions that align with your values and goals. One way to practice mindfulness is to engage in daily meditation. Meditation involves focusing on the breath, body, or a mantra to help quiet the mind and increase awareness of the present moment. Studies have shown that regular meditation can improve focus, increase emotional regulation, and decrease stress, leading to better decision-making. Another way to practice mindfulness is to incorporate mindful habits into your daily routine. For example, taking a few deep breaths before making a decision, or pausing to observe your thoughts and feelings before responding to a situation can help you be more intentional and mindful in your decision-making.

## Understanding Emotional Intelligence

In addition to mindfulness, emotional intelligence is essential for making effective decisions. Emotional intelligence is the ability to recognize, understand, and manage your emotions and also recognize and understand others' emotions. This skill can be particularly useful in decision-making because it allows you to consider not only the facts but the feelings involved.

Practicing self-awareness is one way to develop emotional intelligence. Self-awareness involves paying attention to your thoughts, emotions, and behavior. By increasing your self-awareness, you can better understand your strengths and weaknesses and your emotional triggers and patterns. This understanding can help you make more conscious, intentional decisions that align with your values and goals.

Another way to develop emotional intelligence is to practice empathy. Empathy is the ability to understand and relate to others' emotions and experiences. By developing empathy, you can gain a better understanding of others' perspectives and needs, which can be especially helpful in collaborative decision-making situations.

Optimizing your decision-making process is crucial to success and fulfillment. By understanding how the brain works; learning to overcome common cognitive biases; and optimizing your choices through self-awareness, strategic thinking, and mindfulness, you can make more informed, intentional choices that align with your values and goals.

We can improve our decision-making skills by incorporating daily habits such as meditation, exercise, reading, and journaling. Additionally, seeking feedback, making lists, analyzing past decisions, and trying new experiences can help us develop critical thinking skills and expand our knowledge.

Another key to effective decision-making is approaching it with intention, mindfulness, and a commitment to continuous self-improvement. With practice and patience, anyone can become an expert decision-maker and unlock their full life potential.

One aspect of optimizing our decision-making process is developing creativity. Creativity can help us generate new ideas and perspectives that inform and improve decision-making. Being creative allows us to think differently, consider different viewpoints, and develop innovative solutions.

One way to develop creativity is to engage in activities that encourage it. For example, brainstorming, writing, drawing, or trying new things can help us build a more creative mindset. Additionally, cultivating a sense of curiosity and wonder can also help us develop creativity. We can expand our minds and generate new ideas by approaching life with a sense of wonder and a desire to learn.

By understanding how the brain works, learning to overcome common cognitive biases, and optimizing our choices through self-awareness, strategic thinking, mindfulness, emotional intelligence, and creativity, we can make more informed, intentional choices that align with our values and goals.

We can improve our decision-making abilities through daily practices and habits such as meditation, exercise, reading, journaling, seeking feedback, making lists, and analyzing past decisions. The key is to be intentional and mindful of our choices and continuously work to optimize our decision-making process.

In addition to these daily practices, we can use other specific strategies and techniques to improve decision-making. Let's take a closer look at some of these techniques.

**Use a decision-making framework:** One effective way to make better decisions is to use a decision-making framework, which is a structured approach to making decisions that ensures you consider all relevant factors and weigh them appropriately. Some popular decision-making frameworks include the PROACT method (problem, objectives, alternatives, consequences, trade-offs), the SWOT analysis (strengths, weaknesses, opportunities, threats), and the Cost-Benefit Analysis (weighing the costs against the benefits). Use a framework that can help ensure you make informed and logical decisions.

**Use the 10/10/10 rule:** This technique involves considering how you will feel about your decision in ten minutes, ten months, and ten years. By taking a long-term perspective, you can avoid making impulsive decisions that may provide immediate gratification but could have negative long-term consequences.

**Seek diverse perspectives:** When making important decisions, it's essential to seek out diverse perspectives to ensure you consider all angles of the decision. This could mean getting feedback from colleagues, friends, or family members who have different experiences and viewpoints than you. A variety of viewpoints can help you see the decision from multiple angles and make a more informed choice.

**Avoid decision fatigue:** Decision fatigue is the tendency to make poorer decisions as the day progresses, especially after making many decisions throughout the day. To avoid decision fatigue, consider making essential decisions earlier in the day when your mind is fresh and taking breaks throughout the day to recharge your decision-making abilities.

**Use intuition:** Although we rely on our rational minds to make decisions, intuition can also play an essential role in decision-making. Intuition is our ability to understand something instinctively without needing conscious reasoning. By learning to trust intuition, we can tap into our inner wisdom and make decisions that feel right for us.

**Set deadlines:** Setting deadlines for decision-making can help us avoid analysis paralysis and move forward with a decision. By setting a deadline, you force yourself to weigh the pros and cons and make a choice within a specific period.

**Use a decision journal:** A decision journal is a tool for tracking your decision-making process, including the factors you considered, the decision you made, and the outcome. By keeping a decision journal, you can learn from past choices and avoid making the same mistakes in the future.

These are just a few examples of the many techniques and strategies you can use to optimize decision-making. By combining daily practices and specific procedures, you can improve your ability to make decisions aligned with your goals and values.

One important thing to remember is that decision-making is not an exact science. Even with the best strategies and practices, we will make mistakes and encounter challenges. The key is to remain open-minded, learn from our mistakes, and continuously work to improve our decision-making abilities.

Remember, decision-making is not about making the right choice every time; it's about making the best choice based on your values, goals, and priorities. With a growth mindset and consistent effort, you can train your brain to make better decisions and live a more fulfilling life. So, start optimizing your decision-making skills today by practicing self-awareness, seeking feedback, embracing uncertainty, and cultivating emotional intelligence.

Decision-making is a vital skill that affects every aspect of our lives. We make decisions daily, from mundane to meaningful choices that shape our future. The quality of our decisions determines the quality of our lives. That's why it's crucial to continually develop and optimize our decision-making abilities. By understanding the cognitive neuroscience behind decision-making and using techniques such as conditioning, critical thinking, and emotional intelligence, we can make better decisions and create a better life.

The key is to start with self-awareness and clarity about your values and goals. You can evaluate your choices effectively when you know what you want to achieve. Then, you can apply various strategies such as slowing down, practicing mindfulness, and seeking feedback to make informed and intentional decisions. Remember, every choice you make counts, and it's never too late to optimize your decision-making abilities. With patience and dedication, you can improve your decision-making skills and unlock the full potential of your life.

Don't forget that making effective decisions is not just about making the right choice; it's about making the best choice based on your values, goals, and priorities. Use the daily practices and habits mentioned in this chapter to train your brain to consistently make better decisions. By doing so, you'll be well on your way to living a more fulfilling and purposeful life.

## Self-Reflection

Take the time to answer the questions below using a paper or electronic journal. This process can be incredibly valuable in helping you think through your past decisions and how you might approach decision-making differently in the future. Research indicates writing down your thoughts and recording your decision-making steps helps you retain more information, making it more likely you will remember what you've learned and apply it to your life. Many people read books about self-improvement and positive life changes but never implement the ideas. Your willingness to do the work and answer these questions can be the difference between just reading about improving your decision-making skills and making meaningful changes.

## Questions to Reflect On

- What decision have you made in the past that you now regret? What did you learn from that experience, and how can you apply that knowledge to future decisions?

- How do your core values and long-term goals influence your decision-making?

- Have you made decisions that did not align with your core values, goals, and objectives? Could you have made a better choice?

- Have you ever decided based on short-term gains rather than long-term outcomes? What was the result, and how could you have approached the situation differently?

- Identify three long-term goals or priorities and how your daily decisions could align with them.

- How might you apply the concept of daily conditioning to improve your decision-making process?

- What are some benefits of becoming comfortable with uncertainty in decision-making, and how might you develop this skill?

- What have you learned about critical thinking and emotional intelligence that could help you make more informed and intentional choices?

- What would your ideal decision-making process look like, and what steps could you take to move closer to that ideal?

**Summary**

- Slow down and be intentional about decisions.
- Be aware of your cognitive biases and work to mitigate them.
- Set clear goals and priorities aligned with your core values.
- Practice mindfulness to recognize when you are making a decision based on emotions.
- Become comfortable with uncertainty and ask questions to reduce it.
- Seek feedback from others with different perspectives or experiences.
- Challenge your biases and seek new information to develop critical thinking skills.
- Cultivate emotional intelligence by practicing self-awareness, developing empathy, and recognizing emotions in yourself and others.

## Conclusion

Decision-making is critical to success in all areas of life. The human brain makes thousands of decisions daily, many of which are unconscious, driven by our hardwired survival instincts. However, the challenge lies in optimizing our choices by engaging our rational system and counteracting cognitive biases that can lead to impulsive decisions.

The key to achieving optimal decision-making lies in self-awareness, critical thinking, and emotional intelligence. By conditioning ourselves, becoming comfortable with uncertainty, practicing mindful thinking, being open to feedback, and taking action, we can make more informed, intentional choices that align with our values and goals.

The road to optimal decision-making requires a willingness to put in the effort, consistently reflect and learn from past decisions, and commit to continuous self-improvement. Doing so can unleash our full potential and help us achieve success, happiness, and fulfillment.

# UNLEASHING YOUR OWN POTENTIAL

with Robert Henry

# 2

# DEFINING YOUR OWN DESTINY: THRIVING DESPITE ADVERSITY

*"Character cannot be developed in ease and quiet. Only through experience of trial and suffering can the soul be strengthened, vision cleared, ambition inspired, and success achieved."*

— Helen Keller

My story starts on a US Army base in the picturesque city of Heidelberg, Germany, in early 1973. My father, Don, an Army sergeant, was stationed there, while my mother, Christa, an architecture student, was pursuing her studies at the local university. Their paths would cross in a chance encounter that changed their lives forever.

My mother comes from a family of survivors with a rich history shaped by the aftermath of World War II. Despite the many hardships and difficulties they faced during the war, my grandparents, with their unwavering determination, worked tirelessly to rebuild and create a successful business empire that included farming, real estate, and a variety of other ventures. Their hard work and determination paid off, allowing them to provide their children, including my mother, with the opportunity to get a university education and various work experiences.

Although expectations and discipline were often harsh, from the family farm to the woodshop, my mother and her siblings learned the value of hard work. They never knew their family was wealthy because their parents lived a simple and modest life devoid of ostentation.

My father's childhood was marked by poverty and abuse. Growing up in a large family with ten siblings, he faced many challenges and obstacles. His father, an abusive alcoholic, made the home environment a toxic and dangerous place, leaving my father with little choice but to seek refuge elsewhere.

Joining the Army offered my father a chance to escape the poverty and abuse of his childhood, and he threw himself into his new life with dedication and determination. Despite his rough start, he proved himself to be capable and intelligent, rising to achieve the rank of sergeant.

My father was somewhat of a mystery to me since he worked in Army Intelligence. His path crossed with terrorism in Germany as a bomb exploded in a Jeep parked next to him, leaving him injured. As he was recovering, he met my mother, which changed their lives forever.

One day, my mother and her sister missed their train to the university, and her sister dared her to hitchhike for the first time. As fate would have it, my father picked them up and took them to their destination. The next day, my mother missed her train on purpose, and as if it were meant to be, my father was again the one who picked her up. My father, despite speaking only minimal German, and my mother, who was still learning English, quickly developed a strong connection.

It's incredible to think about how one missed train and a spur-of-the-moment decision led to the start of my parents' story and, ultimately, my existence. This shows that sometimes the most incredible life experiences result from taking a chance and embracing the unknown. They were drawn to each other, leading to their wedding and the birth of yours truly soon in late October of 1973.

As my father regained his strength, he was transferred back to the United States, where the Army deemed him fit for a new assignment. After a brief stop in Michigan, where he had spent his childhood, he was sent to Arizona and assigned to the enigmatic NSA center at Fort Huachuca. This facility, shrouded in secrecy, was a hub for signals intelligence (SIGINT) operations, which was tasked with collecting, analyzing, and decoding foreign communications and electronic signals. As a child, I often wondered what kind of work my father was doing.

In the early 1970s, my mother and father found themselves in an unfamiliar place, far from where either of them had grown up. Sierra Vista was a small town of 10,000 people just fifteen minutes from the busy military hub of Fort Huachuca. Although Sierra Vista is close to exciting destinations such as Sonora, Mexico, and Tucson, Arizona, life was challenging for my parents as they navigated their new environment.

Living in a mobile home park was a significant departure for my mother, who was used to a comfortable lifestyle. Plus, the language barrier made it difficult for her to adjust to her new surroundings. My father's demanding job only added to the stress, causing strain on the marriage.

After serving honorably in the Army, my father chose not to reenlist. They settled in Tucson, Arizona, where he used his Veterans

Administration (VA) benefits to buy a small home. Despite his best intentions to provide my mother with a comfortable life, 1973 brought tough times, with a severe recession, combined with inflation soaring into double digits. The nation's sentiment toward service members was also complicated, with mixed feelings about the Vietnam War and the US military's role in the world.

My father took on various jobs in the food and hospitality industry, and worked his way up to become a general manager of a hotel restaurant. However, his long work hours caused my mother to feel increasingly lonely and unhappy. The distance between them grew, leading to increased tension. Sadly, just before my sister was born in 1977, my father left. My mother was heartbroken and vulnerable. Imagine being a twenty-two-old woman, far from home in a foreign land, eight months pregnant and caring for a four-year-old boy, only to have your husband drop the bombshell that he's leaving.

The mix of fear, heartbreak, and anger that must have flooded my mother is hard to fathom. My father walked away, leaving her to shoulder all the responsibilities, never offering a helping hand or contributing to child support. As I reflect on those years from a distance, it becomes crystal clear why bitterness was a constant companion for my mother throughout my childhood.

The struggles my mother encountered were truly remarkable. She had left behind her aspirations of becoming an architect in Germany by following my father to the United States. Upon arrival, she found herself in a foreign land with limited language skills and no viable career prospects. Nevertheless, she persevered and took a job as a server at a restaurant that later became a Denny's. The task of providing for her young family fell solely on her shoulders, and she had to make difficult choices to ensure our survival.

Childcare was a constant concern, and she was forced to find the most cost-effective solution, often leaving us in less-than-ideal situations. My mother's determination to provide for her children was unwavering, even when faced with the harsh realities of being a young, single mother in a time of financial uncertainty. She worked long hours, often taking on multiple jobs, just to feed and house us.

While my mother struggled to make ends meet in the mid-1980s, she happened to befriend a devout woman who belonged to an unconventional religious community, the Jehovah's Witnesses. Perhaps their initial connection resulted from the woman also being from Germany. As an eight-year-old, I was too young to understand the complexities and nuances of the situation—all I knew was my mother had found a friend who offered us a much-needed escape from the difficulties of everyday life. The highlight of our visits to this woman's home was the chance to dip in the refreshing waters of her pool, a welcome respite from the unrelenting sun in the scorching southern Arizona landscape.

However, this newfound friendship and the religious community it brought us into would soon prove to be both a source of comfort and pain. While the woman was kind and compassionate, her beliefs and practices were extreme, and our association with her and her community would spark even more challenges in the years to come.

It was a difficult time for my mother as she grappled with finding comfort within her newfound faith even as she was rejected by many in the community. Nevertheless, her friend was a source of unwavering support and encouragement, and their bond was long lasting. As a young boy, I may not have fully grasped the significance of this period in my mother's life, but looking back, I can see how it shaped her in ways none of us imagined.

As I watched my mother navigate the challenges of single parenthood, I couldn't help but observe her growing dependence on a religious community vastly different from any she had known. To her, it represented a sanctuary—a place of refuge and safety in an often-uncaring world. The members offered her comfort and a sense of belonging, and she eagerly immersed herself in their teachings and practices.

At first, our weekly attendance at their gatherings seemed harmless enough, but as time passed, I couldn't help but feel uneasy. The community's influence on our lives was becoming increasingly pronounced, and my mother seemed to have blind trust in their every word and deed. It was as if this religious group had taken over our lives, slowly but surely infiltrating every aspect of our existence.

I noticed a sinister pattern—the community's teachings emphasized obedience and subservience, and their practices seemed designed to control and manipulate. They encouraged my mother to seek their assistance in all aspects of her life, from practical matters like home repair to more personal concerns like which doctors to see and an insistence on shunning and avoiding family members not involved in the faith. As I grew older, the community's hold on my mother and desire for power and control seemed cult-like. Their influence on us was insidious, and it seemed my mother was caught in their web, unable to break free from their grasp. I felt a sense of hopelessness and helplessness I couldn't shake.

In 1983, at the tender ages of six and ten, my sister and I found ourselves in the care of another single mother from the same religious community because my mother needed childcare while she worked. This woman would look after us before and after school. Initially, we were excited because the mother had two teenage sons we thought would be great playmates. However, it took only a little while to realize our situation's reality was far from what we had imagined it would be.

This mother was bitter and resentful; her husband had recently left her to fend for herself and her children. To make ends meet, she agreed to take care of us, but it was clear she did not welcome the responsibility. She spent most of her time in her bedroom, watching soap operas or sleeping, leaving my sister and me unsupervised. The once-exciting prospect of being in a new environment with other kids had turned bleak.

The two brothers began molesting me. At ten years old, I wasn't entirely sure what was happening, just that it wasn't right. The teenage boys threatened me to keep me from saying anything to anyone. They explained that what they were doing was just something only boys do. I was scared and ashamed. I was unsure how my mother would react, so I never told her. I was afraid she would not believe me or that, somehow, I would be blamed.

My mother eventually stopped taking us to that home. Although I was filled with relief at the prospect of not having to visit the two teenage brothers again, my fear and shame lingered because I would occasionally see them at religious functions. The trauma they inflicted and the fear of discovery would overwhelm me with a sense of dread and unease every time I laid eyes on them. The thought of revisiting the darkest moments of my childhood filled me with a profound sense of discomfort, causing me to grapple with a range of intense emotions.

Growing up, I often wondered about the complexities of my mother's emotions and the reasons behind her anger and bitterness. Her childhood was marked by strict and demanding parents who had lost everything during World War II and worked tirelessly to rebuild their fortunes. They were known for their high expectations and harsh punishments for anything less than perfection from their children. This childhood experience shaped my mother's perceptions of life and love, and she seemed to have a fairytale notion of what her marriage to my father would entail.

However, reality soon set in, and the marriage was far from perfect. My mother struggled with the disappointment and disillusionment of her failed expectations, and her sadness gradually turned to bitterness. I often wondered if this bitterness played a role in my father's decision to leave us—it was a question that lingered in my mind for many years. My mother's relationship with her parents and how it shaped her life has always remained a topic of intrigue and contemplation for me.

As a child, I couldn't help noticing how she often connected me to my father, and people frequently commented on how much I resembled him. This connection seemed to trigger my mother's anger and frustration. Although I now realize she loved me in her way, or the only way she knew, our relationship was marked by a palpable tension with little room for affection or tenderness.

Like her parents had for her, my mother had high expectations of me that were matched only by the ferocity of her punishments. These often took the form of brutal beatings with a wooden spoon or a length of garden hose. The beatings led to frequent visits from the police and Child Protective Services, often triggered by concerned teachers, counselors, or neighbors who had overheard the violence. These experiences left me in a lifelong struggle to process the love and affection so sparingly given and the lingering scars of a childhood spent under the shadow of violence and shame.

As I entered middle school in 1986, a young man of twenty-two came into our lives, bringing excitement and intrigue. This enigmatic figure had newly become involved in our religious community, and he seemed to take a keen interest in me. At thirteen, I was flattered by his attention, and he even taught me racquetball. However, as the days passed, I began to sense his true intention was to ingratiate himself with my mother, a single parent raising two children.

I couldn't blame my mother for being drawn to him. Being a thirty-year-old woman, my mother must have been swept off her feet by the attention of a young and handsome man nearly a decade her junior. Given the religious doctrine of abstinence before marriage, their relationship blossomed rapidly into marriage. The thought of a man so much younger with a life so different from hers capturing her heart must have been a thrilling prospect, but I couldn't help wondering about the many complexities of this unique relationship.

The young man's sudden appearance in our lives was a turning point for my family, and his influence would have lasting effects on all of us.

The memory of their wedding day still haunts me. I recall the chill that ran down my spine when my stepfather took me aside and told me our household was about to change dramatically. He warned me I had better learn to respect him as the head of the house or I would face the consequences. To my horror, I soon discovered he was not bluffing.

As the days passed, I watched in despair as my mother assumed a subservient role in the household, deferring to my stepfather on even the most trivial matters. The tension between us continued to escalate as he repeatedly attempted to assert his position of authority and dominance over me. Together, they tended to adopt the most stringent interpretations of our religious doctrines, dictating every aspect of our lives, from the clothes we wore to the people we associated with. I was forbidden to participate in any school activities or sports and was even prohibited from having a girlfriend, a crushing blow for a young teenager starting to explore the world around him.

Feeling suffocated by these restrictions and the poverty plaguing our household, I decided to get a job. A member of our religious community owned a janitorial business, and much to my surprise, my mother and stepfather agreed to let me work there. I was overjoyed at the chance to escape the suffocating atmosphere of our home, so I threw myself into my work. The man I worked for was a true inspiration, a self-made success. He worked tirelessly to provide for his family. He cleaned offices and supermarkets at night while running a construction business during the day. He had even built the home he shared with his wife and two young boys.

When I turned fifteen, I felt optimistic about my future. I could finally afford new school clothes and began to save for a car, imagining the freedom and independence it would bring. However, my stepfather had other plans. One day, he said I had to start contributing by paying 25 percent of the household expenses since I considered myself an adult. I was devastated, especially since I was already doing many household chores, including laundry, dishes, vacuuming, and yard work. When I tried to explain this to him, he berated me, saying he was the man of the house, and I should listen to him without question. This expense took more than 90 percent of my income.

That intense moment still plays in my mind on a never-ending loop. I feel the weight of my lack of courage to this day. At fifteen, I was already much bigger and stronger than my stepfather, yet I lacked the fortitude to stand up to him and defend myself. The memory of that day serves as a haunting reminder of the power dynamics in our household and the toll they took on me as a young, impressionable teenager.

Amid the monotony and suffocating restrictions of my home life, a ray of light appeared in the form of a new family moving into our neighborhood. With them came a captivating and striking teenage daughter, Lesley, who, to my great delight, would be attending the same high school as me. I was instantly smitten. My heart beat faster at the mere sight of her, and I felt an immediate connection. However, we were both too shy to express our feelings openly.

As the days passed, we found ourselves in a few classes together and gradually grew more at ease around each other. I'd walk with her from school, even though it took us in the opposite direction of my home, to bask in her presence and steal a few moments of conversation. The religious gatherings we attended twice a week were filled with nervous glances, stilted dialogue, and awkward attempts to hide our growing attraction.

Despite our religious community's strict rules and expectations, I found myself drawn to her in ways I couldn't explain. As our friendship blossomed, I felt myself coming alive. My days were no longer filled with drudgery and despair but excitement and anticipation. Our attraction grew stronger by the day, and I knew I was falling in love. It was new and intoxicating, unlike anything I had ever felt.

And so, with each passing day, I fell deeper and deeper under her spell, desperate to find a way to tell her how I felt. But the fears and constraints of our religious community loomed large, and we knew our relationship would never be accepted.

One night, the thrill of young love ignited and I snuck out of my quiet home, hopping onto my faithful bicycle for a secret rendezvous with my love. I was excited as I rode toward her window under the glittering night sky. When I finally arrived, we whispered sweet nothings to each other and talked about everything our strict homes and religion wouldn't let us do.

Time seemed to stand still as we became lost in the moment, sharing tender kisses on a cozy patio set beneath the starry sky. As the first light of dawn began to break across the Arizona sky, we reluctantly parted.

Before I could even make it home, tragedy struck. A woman ran a stop sign a few blocks from my house. I was going too fast to stop or avoid hitting her. My pedal hit her rear bumper, and I was sent soaring over the top of the handlebars. The next thing I remember was coming to and realizing I couldn't see anything in front of me, only in my peripheral vision. The car had taken off, leaving me to pick up my bike and walk the remaining few blocks home.

When I got home, I put my bike away as quietly as possible and quickly went into the bathroom to assess the damage. I couldn't see anything I looked at directly and had to take side-long glances at myself. I went to my sister's bedroom—she was only twelve at the time—to get her help. I had to get cleaned up and into bed before our parents woke up.

When I gently shook my sister awake, her response told me how serious my injury was. She slowly opened her eyes and then shrieked uncontrollably when she focused on my face. My right temple, where I'd hit the ground, looked like it had exploded. Her first thought was I'd been shot. When I managed to quiet her down, she began to fear our parents had done something drastic to me. She still tells me how terrified she was at the time.

My mother was roused by the noise and came into the room. She made me sit on the vinyl floor to avoid getting blood anywhere. Then she wrapped my head in a towel and took me to the emergency room. Thankfully, her husband was working nights and not home, or the scene would have been much more complicated. After a few stitches and some admonition to watch out for my concussion, we went home to find my stepfather waiting pensively.

I made up some cockamamie story about coming home from work, feeling amped up, and taking my bike for a ride to burn off some energy. I'm sure they didn't buy it, but I stuck to my story. They made me get ready to go to a religious meeting we attended every Sunday, and I didn't object because my girlfriend would also be there—I would be proud to show off the wounds I got from sneaking out to see her.

The Elders of our community soon caught wind of my secret romance. I was called into a small, stuffy back room and surrounded by three of them; I couldn't help feeling fear and anger. Just a few weeks before, I had been caught up in the rush of first love, sneaking out under cover of night to spend time with my girlfriend. Now I was facing judgment from the people who were supposed to guide and support me on my faith journey.

The Elders drilled me with questions. Their voices were stern and uncompromising when they warned me about the dangers of dating and the consequences of premarital sex. As they spoke, I could feel their hypocrisy radiating from them. After all, two of the three Elders in the room had teenage children rumored to be dating and possibly even engaging in premarital sex.

The tension was palpable. Despite their attempts to intimidate me, I refused to back down. I was determined to protect my girlfriend and our relationship and wouldn't let anyone else dictate our path. I held my tongue and stuck to my story, even as the Elders pressed me for information.

In the end, although relieved it was finally over, I left feeling a strange mix of emotions—defiance but also sadness because it was hard to understand how these people could be so hypocritical in their words and actions. Yet at the same time, I was encouraged by the strength I'd gained from standing true to myself despite external pressure.

Back at home, the suffocating tension escalated with each passing day. My movements were even more restricted than before. My stepfather grounded me for a grueling two weeks. Anger and frustration boiled inside me, and I couldn't help but challenge him. "Why not just make it a month?" I said. "After all, even when I'm not grounded, it's not much different."

I could feel his rage simmering as he tried to force me to sit in the corner of the entryway as punishment for my defiance. I looked over at my mother, searching for any shred of support, but she looked away. I refused to be reduced to a little child and stood my ground, taunting my stepfather to take a swing. I was sixteen at the time, but at six-foot-two I felt like a giant compared to his frail frame. He must have realized we were teetering on the brink of a physical altercation because he backed down, but not before warning my mother, "This has to stop."

The next day, after school, I walked over to a run-down strip of apartments that looked like a sketchy halfway house or drug rehab center. I had saved enough money for a couple of months' rent, and the manager, seeing the opportunity to make a quick buck, agreed to rent me a studio with no questions asked. I felt a sense of liberation, knowing this would be a big step toward gaining control of my life.

That evening, I went home and announced my intentions. I was going to pursue one of two options within a week. I was either going to move into the apartment or move to Los Angeles to live with my father. My mother and stepfather laughed at the thought of me moving to California, insisting my father wouldn't want to deal with me. But I was determined to take control of my life, so I picked up the phone and called my father. I'll never forget the sound of his voice as he exclaimed in disbelief, "You want to move in with me? Of course, I welcome you!"

As much as I yearned to escape the suffocating environment I was in, leaving my girlfriend behind weighed heavily on my mind. My mother and stepfather insisted they would decide what I was going to do, but I had made up my mind. I was done living in their bizarre home, done being treated like a child. I turned away from them, not wanting to hear any more of their objections, and got ready for work. I knew the next few days would be critical, and I was determined to make the right choice for my future.

That night, after working one of my longest shifts, the quiet of the night felt almost suffocating. Despite my exhaustion, I couldn't resist sneaking over to my girlfriend's house for a quick visit. We spent a few hours together, laughing and chatting, unaware it would be the last time we'd see each other for two decades.

As I made my way home and finally drifted off to sleep, eyes heavy with exhaustion, I couldn't have imagined the whirlwind about to hit me. My door burst open, and lights flooded the room. My stepfather stood there, his face stern and unyielding, as he tossed a suitcase on my bed. "Get packed!" he barked. "We leave in an hour. Take only what you need." I was utterly taken aback, struggling to understand what was happening. My mother's face was expressionless, offering no clues or comfort. Only my sister eventually filled me in. They had purchased a bus ticket for me to move to Los Angeles and live with my father. I was just shy of seventeen.

Before I even had a chance to process the news, I was on a Greyhound bus to Phoenix and then a flight to Los Angeles. My head was swirling with conflicting emotions. I was leaving behind everything I had ever known—my home, my sister, a few friends, and my girlfriend. I felt more alone and vulnerable than I ever had before.

The miles flew past, and as the Greyhound bus made its way to Phoenix and then on to Los Angeles, I couldn't help feeling a sense of disbelief. Just a few hours earlier, I had been living my everyday life, and now I was on a journey to an entirely new and unknown future. But a tiny spark of hope and excitement remained despite the fear and uncertainty threatening to overcome me. I couldn't help but wonder about the future.

Arriving in Los Angeles in 1990, I was struck by my father's transformation. Four years had passed since I last saw him, and the change was startling. He appeared severely aged, having lost much weight, leading me to suspect a serious health issue like AIDS, known for its drastic effects. This possibility stirred a tumultuous mix of emotions within me, ranging from fear to shame and guilt. The thought of my father grappling with such a condition was both frightening and hard to believe. Yet, the evidence was unmistakably present, confronting me with a reality that intertwined fear, shame, and guilt in a daunting, poignant blend.

On the one hand, I felt shame for even considering the possibility of my father having AIDS. It felt like a betrayal as if I suspected him of doing something wrong. But I couldn't ignore the signs that pointed to the advanced stages of the disease.

In the early 1990s, the public's understanding of AIDS was limited, and the disease was often shrouded in fear and misinformation. People with AIDS were frequently stigmatized and discriminated against, making it difficult for them to find housing, employment, and proper medical care. The misconceptions about casual transmission of the disease left many viewing those with AIDS as morally suspect and dangerous.

When Magic Johnson, a high-profile basketball star, revealed he was living with HIV, it marked a significant change in public perception of the disease. Johnson's courageous act of going public with his diagnosis brought increased awareness to the issue of AIDS and helped dispel many myths and misconceptions surrounding it. He became a powerful advocate for people living with AIDS and worked tirelessly to raise awareness and improve their quality of life.

My mother's accusations of my father leaving her for a gay relationship continued to resonate in my thoughts. Even though he had disclosed to me that he had pancreatic cancer, my suspicions persisted due to the visible decline in his health. While I now lean toward believing he ultimately succumbed to AIDS, I refrained from directly confronting my father about his condition.

The thought that my father may have been one of the people affected by the disease was overwhelming. I couldn't help but wonder if that was why he had come to Los Angeles—to access better healthcare. The conflicting emotions I was feeling were almost too much to bear. I was torn between my loyalty to my father, my concern for his well-being, and my fear about the disease and its stigma. AIDS or not, my father's condition was a heavy weight to bear, but I was determined to be there for him and support him in any way I could. After all, it wasn't as if I could turn around and head back home.

Living in Palmdale, a Los Angeles suburb, with my father, his wife Cora, and their blended family stirred up a whirlwind of conflicting emotions. Cora had an adult daughter named Kimberly, and together, she and my father had another daughter named Kourtney. The adjustment was not easy. My arrival made the three-bedroom apartment, which now housed a family of five, seem tight. However, I was determined to make the best of the situation and create strong bonds with my new family.

One of the most noticeable changes that caught my attention was my stepmother's transformation. I had met her once years earlier. Now, the once lively and energetic woman appeared tired, worn-out, and aged far beyond her years. Although she still radiated love and affection toward me, the sadness in her eyes was palpable, as if rooted in something much more profound. She completed her daily tasks with a sense of urgency, as if she were constantly racing against time. The weight of caring for my father, who was no longer able to work because of his illness, and running their janitorial business seemed to be taking its toll on her.

The fear that my father might not have much time left lingered in the back of my mind, and the possibility that he was living with AIDS was a constant source of concern. The emotions that came with this situation were overwhelming, and it wasn't easy to wrap my head around the thoughts. I threw myself into my new surroundings, striving to build strong relationships with my siblings, help around the house, and support my stepmother in running their janitorial business. I refused to let the fear and unknowns control my thoughts and actions.

As my father's health worsened with each passing day, I felt an immense responsibility to be by his side and do everything possible to make his final moments as comfortable and peaceful as possible. This became my daily routine, driving to the VA hospital in Sepulveda, spending countless hours sitting beside him, watching as he slowly slipped away from me. The journey from the hospital back to the offices of my father's janitorial customers, where I still had cleaning duties to complete, proved to be both emotionally and physically draining. However, I was determined not to leave my father's side until I absolutely had to. It was heartbreaking to watch my father slowly slip away. I had only just reconnected with him after so many years, and now our precious few months together were tarnished by the sight of him in decline. The thought that I would never see his smile, hear his laughter, or feel his embrace again was a constant ache in my heart.

One day, my father's younger brother, Uncle David, arrived from across the country to offer his support and spend time with my father. He suggested I take a break to rest, and I reluctantly agreed, knowing he needed one-on-one time with his brother. Feeling physically and emotionally drained, I decided to leave my uncle at the VA hospital with my dad. I went home, hoping to get some much-needed rest, with the thought that my father's condition might improve by the time I returned to the hospital in a day or two. The next morning, my stepmother woke me in tears. I knew immediately what had happened. Realizing my father was gone was like a physical blow. The guilt of not being by his side in his final moments weighed heavily on me, and the pain of losing my father so soon after being reunited with him was unbearable. Those last few months of heartbreak and decline would be the primary memories I had of my father, and they would haunt me forever.

February 11, 1991—the day my father passed away—was filled with heartbreak and sadness, and it remains one of the saddest days of my life. My father was a flawed man with many imperfections who had made many mistakes, and for a long time, I struggled to reconcile his shortcomings with my love and admiration for him. He was not the ideal father my sister and I deserved, and he deeply regretted it. He knew he had let us down, and I could see the pain and sadness in his eyes every time we visited him at the VA hospital.

Despite his flaws, my father was a proud veteran who had served our country honorably. I will never forget him as a man who loved his country and was willing to put his life on the line to protect it. Attending his funeral at Riverside National Cemetery was an emotional experience. I watched as the honor guard from March Air Reserve Base presented the flag to my stepmother and fired a rifle salute. The sound of "Taps," a mournful tune played on a bugle, still sends chills down my spine and brings me to tears. It was a fitting farewell to a man who had served our country with distinction and symbolized our deep appreciation and gratitude for our nation's heroes.

Although my father had many shortcomings and imperfections, I could still feel his love and affection during those brief moments when he was present and engaged with me. His passing left a deep void in my life that can never be filled. I will be haunted by his memory for the rest of my life.

As we returned home, I faced a complex and seemingly impossible decision. My stepmother planned to move to Michigan, close to her family. I was only seventeen and had to choose between going with her, attempting to build a life on my own in a Los Angeles suburb, or calling my mother to ask if I could return to Arizona. I was in turmoil as I struggled to decide what my best path forward was.

Staying in Palmdale was a defining moment for me. It was a moment of both uncertainty and resolve. As my stepmother drove away, she left me with just a hundred and fifty dollars in my pocket and a burning desire to make my own way. I took on the challenge with everything I had. I rented a room from a neighbor and took on three grueling jobs, working tirelessly every day to make a life for myself. My hard work and dedication paid off. A year later, I was able to purchase a car and move into a little apartment of my own, taking my first step toward independence.

Finding myself alone in Southern California, with few acquaintances to lean on, I began attending the local Jehovah's Witnesses Kingdom Hall sporadically, almost as a way to find some semblance of familiarity in a new place. Little did I know this decision would introduce me to two remarkable individuals, reshaping my life once again.

Patricia was a young woman whose father had been left quadriplegic by a bicycle accident eight years prior. We immediately bonded over our shared experiences of caring for our respective fathers, and our conversations often veered toward our disillusionment with the religion we were part of. Patricia was a burst of energy, radiating vivacity. At the time, she was pursuing a career as a nursing assistant.

I also met Shane, a paint store general manager, who initially hired me as a driver but soon recognized my potential. He became my mentor, guiding me into the sales manager role. This transition marked a significant step into adulthood, enhanced by forming diverse connections with contractors throughout Southern California. Alongside this professional journey, my romance with Patricia gradually faded, leaving me in solitude. Feeling isolated, my yearning for Tucson, Arizona, my hometown, intensified. I eventually packed my life into suitcases filled with hope and determination. Thus, I embarked on a journey back to Tucson, eager to start a new chapter in life.

## Defining Your Destiny Despite Adversity

Adversity is an inevitable part of life. As we journey through life, we will encounter setbacks, disappointments, and obstacles. However, how we react to adversity makes us who we are. Overcoming adversity and thriving despite it is not easy, but it is possible. Some of the most successful people in the world have overcome significant adversity to achieve their goals. Like Nick Vujicic, born without limbs, countless examples exist of individuals who have defined their destinies and thrived despite adversity.

The ability to overcome adversity and thrive in the face of difficulty requires a combination of mindset, purpose, resilience, and support. By adopting a growth mindset, cultivating a strong sense of purpose, developing resilience, and building a support network, we can overcome adversity and define our destinies.

## Developing a Growth Mindset

Let's start with mindset. When we face challenges or setbacks, it is easy to feel defeated and helpless. We may feel like giving up or believe the odds are stacked against us. But remember, the obstacle does not define us; how we respond to the obstacle defines us. How we choose to move forward determines our success.

A growth mindset is a powerful belief in the potential for your abilities and intelligence to develop through hard work, perseverance, and a willingness to learn from failures. It transforms challenges into opportunities for personal growth, shifting your focus from mere outcomes to the process of learning itself. Embracing a growth mindset equips you with the resilience to face obstacles head-on, viewing them as steppingstones rather than impassable barriers.

The practice of a growth mindset unlocks a world of potential, allowing you to recognize opportunities for growth in every endeavor. It encourages you to fully engage in the learning process, fostering a proactive approach to your own success. This mentality empowers you to take charge of your journey, confident in your ability to navigate the path ahead.

In her influential book *Mindset: The New Psychology of Success*, psychologist Carol Dweck, a trusted authority in motivation and mindset, underscores the profound significance of a growth mindset. She emphasizes, "The passion for stretching yourself and sticking to it, even (or especially) when it's not going well, is the hallmark of the growth mindset." Based on the wisdom of Dweck's research and insights, adopting a growth mindset becomes a transformative journey, instilling in you the confidence and optimism needed to conquer any obstacle that comes your way. Carol Dweck's work stands as a beacon of guidance and a testament to the power of cultivating a growth-oriented perspective.

One key to cultivating a growth mindset is focusing on the progress you make rather than the setbacks you encounter. You can start by identifying your strengths and weaknesses, setting realistic goals, and taking small steps toward achieving them. It's essential to remain persistent, even when things don't go according to plan.

Another critical aspect of developing a growth mindset is embracing failure as a part of the learning process. As author, podcast host, and motivational speaker Mel Robbins once said, "You are not a failure unless you quit." When you adopt this mindset, you'll see failures as valuable opportunities to learn and grow rather than as reasons to give up.

At the same time, it's essential to surround yourself with positive influences, such as mentors and like-minded individuals who can support you and provide constructive feedback. Positive thinking and self-talk can also go a long way toward developing a growth mindset. As Norman Vincent Peale, pastor and author of *The Power of Positive Thinking*, once said, "Change your thoughts, and you change your world."

A growth mindset is the foundation of success. A growth mindset can be your superpower, enabling you to overcome tall obstacles and achieve your goals. Remember, the obstacle does not define you—how you respond to the obstacle does.

## Focusing on Your Purpose

In addition to a growth mindset, cultivating a strong sense of purpose is critical for thriving in the face of adversity. When we have a clear sense of purpose, we are more likely to persevere through challenges and setbacks. Purpose gives us direction and meaning and helps us stay focused on our goals even when things get tough.

Buddha said, "Your purpose in life is to find your purpose and give your whole heart and soul to it." And President Kennedy said, "Efforts and courage are not enough without purpose and direction." When we find and live according to our purpose, we tap into a sense of fulfillment and joy that can help us overcome any obstacle.

So how do we go about discovering our purpose? For some, it may come naturally, but for others, it may take some introspection and soul searching. As professor and author Brené Brown, known for her work on shame, vulnerability, and leadership, once said, "What is worth doing even if I fail?" Asking ourselves this question can help us identify the things that truly matter to us and guide us toward our purpose.

It's also essential to align our purpose with our values and passions. When we do something that aligns with our core values and passions, we tap into a sense of fulfillment and joy that can help us overcome any obstacle that comes our way. Author, marketing executive, and career coach Maya Grossman once said, "You don't have to be great to start, but you have to start to be great."

Another key aspect of developing a strong sense of purpose is to set specific, measurable goals that align with our purpose. When we set goals that align with our purpose, we stay focused on our path and are more likely to persevere through challenges and setbacks. One of the greatest personal development experts, author and motivational speaker Zig Ziglar, once said, "If you aim at nothing, you will hit it every time."

At the same time, it's essential to remain flexible and adaptable when pursuing our purpose. Life can be unpredictable, and sometimes our path may need to shift or change course. But when we have a strong sense of purpose, we can adapt to the changing circumstances and continue moving forward toward our goals.

Cultivating a strong purpose is crucial for overcoming adversity and achieving success. When we have a clear sense of purpose, we can stay focused on our goals, tap into a sense of fulfillment and joy, and persevere through any difficulties that come our way. So, take the time to discover your purpose, align it with your values and passions, set specific goals, remain adaptable, and enjoy the journey toward ultimate success.

## Fine-Tuning Your Resiliency

Developing resilience is one of the best ways to face and overcome challenges. Resilience is the ability to bounce back from adversity and adapt and thrive in the face of change and challenge. We are not born with resilience—it is a skill we can develop and strengthen over time, and we need to be intentional about doing so.

Practicing self-care is an effective way of cultivating resiliency. Adversity can take a toll on our physical, emotional, and mental health, so it's crucial to take care of ourselves to better cope with life's challenges. Getting enough sleep, exercise, and proper nutrition can help us feel more energized and better equipped to face adversity. Additionally, practicing mindfulness, meditation, or other stress-reducing techniques can help us manage our emotions and focus on our goals.

It is vital to avoid getting trapped in negative thought patterns when we face adversity. Negative self-talk, rumination, and catastrophizing can make it harder to bounce back from setbacks and contribute to feelings of hopelessness and despair. Instead, try to reframe your thoughts in a more positive and constructive way. For example, instead of dwelling on what went wrong, focus on what you can learn from the experience and how you can move forward.

Moreover, cultivating resiliency means being willing to take risks and fail. We can develop resiliency and overcome adversity by taking risks and pushing ourselves outside of our comfort zones. It's essential to recognize that failure is not the end but a steppingstone to success. Prolific author and prominent personal development expert Seth Godin once said, "The cost of being wrong is less than the cost of doing nothing."

It is crucial to remain flexible and adaptable when faced with change or adversity. Life can be unpredictable, and sometimes our path may need to shift. But when we are resilient, we can adapt to the changing circumstances and continue moving toward our goals. As author, modern Stoic, and public-relations strategist Ryan Holiday once said, "The obstacle is the way."

Developing resiliency is critical to success. By practicing self-care, reframing negative thoughts, taking risks, and remaining flexible, we can develop resiliency and overcome adversity. In Zig Ziglar's words, "It's not what happens to you that determines how far you will go in life; it is how you handle what happens to you."

## Building Your Support Network

Another key to thriving in the face of adversity is to develop a strong support network. As we navigate the unpredictable waters of life, the support of a strong network of individuals who believe in us, who are willing to stand by us through thick and thin, can make all the difference. Developing a strong support network is important in building resilience and overcoming adversity. Not only can these individuals provide us with much-needed emotional support, but they can also help us find solutions to our problems and encourage us to pursue our goals and aspirations.

One of the best ways to develop a strong support network is to actively seek out individuals who share our values, interests, and goals. This search might include joining a community organization, volunteering for a charity, or participating in a recreational activity or club. By doing so, we put ourselves in contact with like-minded individuals who can offer us much-needed support, motivation, and guidance.

It's also important to recognize that building a support network is not one-sided. To truly benefit from the support of others, we must also be willing to offer our support. This means being a good listener, providing encouragement and motivation, and lending a helping hand when needed. By taking an active role in supporting our friends and family, we strengthen our relationships and build a stronger support network that can help us overcome even the most challenging situations.

Communication is one of the most important aspects of building a strong support network. It's essential to communicate with the people in our network in an open and honest way, sharing our struggles and triumphs and being willing to listen to their experiences. By doing so, we can gain valuable insights and perspectives, learn new strategies for coping with stress and adversity, and build a deeper connection with those around us.

In addition to actively seeking support, it's also important to create a supportive environment in our own lives. This might include setting boundaries, practicing self-care, and seeking resources to help us manage stress and anxiety. By taking care of ourselves, we show others we value our well-being, and we are better equipped to support others.

Building a strong support network requires effort, communication, and commitment. By seeking individuals who share our values and interests, being willing to offer our support, and creating a supportive environment, we can build a network of people who can help us overcome even the most daunting of challenges. Remember, you are not alone, and there is always someone who cares and is willing to listen. So, reach out, build connections, and know that we can overcome even the toughest challenges together.

Ultimately, thriving in the face of adversity requires a combination of mindset, purpose, resilience, and support. By adopting a growth mindset, cultivating a strong sense of purpose, developing resilience, and building a support network, we can overcome adversity and define our future.

**Self-Reflection**

To truly benefit from the material covered in this chapter, I invite you to take a few minutes to answer the following thought-provoking questions related to the material you have just read. By writing out your answers, you will be able to internalize and apply what you have learned. This will provide you with new tools and ways of facing adversity, and it will provoke changes in how you handle future adversity. Remember, real progress comes from taking action, so grab a pen and let's get started.

## Questions to Reflect On

- How has adversity helped shape who you are today, and what positive lessons have you learned from those experiences?
- What steps can you take to cultivate a strong support network, and how can you strengthen those relationships during adversity?
- How have negative thought patterns or self-talk held you back in the face of challenges, and how can you reframe those thoughts to be more positive and constructive?
- How can developing a growth mindset and a sense of purpose help you build resilience and overcome adversity?
- Which self-care practices do you currently use to help cope with adversity, and how can you incorporate additional practices to better support your physical, emotional, and mental health?
- What actions can you take to support others facing adversity, and how can you strengthen your support network by offering help to others?

## Summary

- Develop a growth mindset by believing your abilities and intelligence can be developed through hard work, persistence, and a willingness to learn from failure. Embrace challenges as opportunities for growth, and learn to focus on the process of learning rather than just the outcome.

- Cultivate a strong sense of purpose by finding and living according to your values and goals. This will give you direction and meaning and help you stay focused on your objectives even in tough times.

- Build resilience by developing a support network of friends, family, mentors, or support groups. Having people who believe in you, encourage you, and are there for you when you need them can help you bounce back from adversity.

- Practice self-care to improve your physical, emotional, and mental health. Getting enough sleep, exercise, and proper nutrition can help you feel more energized and better equipped to face adversity. Additionally, practicing mindfulness, meditation, or other stress-reducing techniques can help you manage your emotions and focus on your goals.

- Avoid getting trapped in negative thought patterns by reframing your thoughts more positively and constructively. Instead of dwelling on what went wrong, focus on what you can learn from the experience and how you can move forward.

- Support others facing adversity and strengthen your support network by offering help to others. By helping others, you build stronger connections and cultivate a sense of purpose and fulfillment that can help you overcome any obstacle.

## Conclusion

Defining your destiny and thriving despite adversity is possible for anyone, no matter their circumstances. By developing a growth mindset, setting goals, taking action, and never giving up on yourself or your dreams, you can overcome any obstacle and achieve success and fulfillment. Remember, your past does not define your future, and your current circumstances do not determine your destiny. You have the power to define your own destiny and create the life you truly desire.

# UNLEASHING YOUR OWN POTENTIAL

with Robert Henry

# 3

# TAKING CHARGE OF YOUR LIFE: HOW TO BREAK FREE FROM THE GRIP OF CIRCUMSTANCES

*"The greatest glory in living lies not in never falling, but in rising every time we fall."*

— Nelson Mandela

At the age of twenty, returning to Tucson felt like stepping onto familiar ground, a chance to hit the reset button and rebuild my life. My childhood sweetheart had long departed, leaving only a few familiar faces from my past. Despite being back in my hometown, a sense of isolation lingered as I yearned for a place to belong.

Ironically, I ended up moving into a condo just a stone's throw from where my mom and stepdad resided. Oddly enough, even with such proximity, our relationship remained strained. During my time in Southern California, we hadn't interacted much, and upon returning to Tucson, our connection remained distant.

In an attempt to rediscover some sense of belonging, I occasionally attended church events, hoping to reconnect with a few old acquaintances from my childhood. I jumped at the opportunity to take a sales position at a well-known national electronics store. I was drawn to sales because I saw it as an opportunity to grow my income based on my skills and abilities. I was confident my sales and communication skills would only improve with time and experience, and I saw that as a means of building a life.

I threw myself into the role with abandon, determined to be the best salesperson I could be. I spent countless hours studying the latest products, perfecting my pitch, and refining my approach. The hard work paid off, and I rose through the ranks, becoming one of the top salespeople in the company.

One memorable night out with my friends, I crossed paths with Ginger, a remarkable woman who, at twenty-three, was a year older than me. She seemed to be connected to everyone I knew, casting an intriguing aura of mystery around her. Even though we only interacted in group settings, I felt an unexplainable pull toward her. Intrigued and captivated, I took the leap and asked her out.

Our first date marked a turning point in our connection. As we conversed and got to know each other, I was struck by her honesty and openness. Ginger shared with me about her three-year-old son, Zachary, and while the notion of dating a single mother initially gave me pause, her deep love and passion for her child were irresistible. I found myself wondering what it would be like to meet Zachary and become a part of his life.

From the moment I met Zachary, I felt fate had led me to them. With his father absent, I saw an opportunity to make a positive impact on his life. Our bond grew rapidly, and I soon realized what I had been searching for was a sense of family, a connection to something greater than myself. Before long, I proposed to Ginger and her son, for they had wholly captured my heart. Ginger and I were married when I was just twenty-four. Shortly before the wedding, I had a unique sales opportunity at an advertising company. The company was a fresh face in town, offering an alternative to the traditional utility company's phonebook—it was when every household still had a phonebook.

In working with this company's clients, I was immediately intrigued by the prospect of talking to business owners about their marketing strategies and getting a glimpse into the inner workings of their companies. I was fascinated by their stories about how they started, the challenges they faced, and the triumphs they celebrated. Each interaction felt like a chance to learn something new and gain a deeper understanding of the business world.

Spending more and more time talking to business owners about their marketing needs, I noticed a common frustration. With so many different marketing mediums available—newspapers, magazines, phonebooks, billboards, radio, and television—budgeting across multiple platforms was overwhelming. This often led to inefficiency and lack of return on their marketing investments.

I became fascinated with the idea of finding a solution to this challenge. I dove into learning about market demographics and the effectiveness of advertising on various platforms. I realized the key to success was understanding the target audience and the most effective way to reach them.

With this newfound knowledge, I began connecting with sales representatives from all the marketing platforms. I was determined to develop a comprehensive ad program to help business owners maximize their budgets and effectively reach their target audience. I was driven to help them make the most of their advertising efforts and ensure they got the best return on their investments.

I started offering my clients a unique service, a comprehensive ad program customized to their needs and budgets. The program considered the business owners' target audience and the demographics of the market they were trying to reach. By spreading a percentage of their budget across each platform, my clients could achieve maximum effectiveness for their marketing investment. I became known for my ability to help businesses navigate the advertising landscape and make the most of their marketing budget.

I soon found myself among the top five sales reps in the company. The company had branches in five states, and the seventy sales reps in our office were fiercely competitive.

As I built my sales portfolio, I also built strong relationships with a few colleagues with top sales numbers. We became a close-knit group who worked together and celebrated each other's successes. We bounced ideas off each other and provided support during challenging times.

The connections and relationships I built were not just limited to my colleagues. My work gave me the chance to interact with a diverse range of clients, from small business owners to high-level executives. I constantly learned from these interactions, gained new insights into the business world, and built a valuable contacts network. I gained a unique perspective on the business world and the inner workings of the companies I worked with. I was proud to be part of my company's success and help contribute to the growth of so many businesses.

My optimism about a future with this company came crashing down when the corporate office suddenly announced a drastic cut in sales rep compensation. Our earnings were going to take a devastating 40 percent hit overnight.

The five of us leading the pack in sales were dumbfounded and angry. The changes felt like a punch in the gut. We believed the corporate office was intentionally trying to limit our earnings. The sense of security and stability we had built up was replaced by a feeling of betrayal and uncertainty. The corporate world seemed to be saying our hard work and dedication were no longer valued.

The five of us had many intense debates about what to do. We represented a significant portion of our region's sales, home to over seventy sales reps. Our discussions were fueled by our collective ambition and drive to succeed. And as we talked, the seed of an idea began to take root.

We were all well-connected in the advertising industry, with solid relationships and contacts who could prove invaluable in a new venture. We had great work ethics, and we possessed a range of complementary skills that would be invaluable in starting our own advertising company. The idea was irresistible, and soon we were all consumed by it, each of us imagining the possibilities and potential success ahead.

With our minds made up, we planned to finish the selling cycle for the upcoming phone book publication. This would allow us to retain the final commission bonuses we earned from the sales contracts we had already written. Our energy and excitement were palpable as we quietly worked to put our plans in motion. In contrast to our colleagues, who had adopted a defeated demeanor following the company's announcement, we stood out with our excitement and drive.

One day, as I was walking toward the building where I worked, I was abruptly approached by two plainclothes detectives. They informed me, with a sense of gravity and urgency, that they had a warrant for my arrest. My world was turned upside down at that moment. I was overcome by shock.

The detectives were professional and courteous, but the situation was still incredibly embarrassing as they cuffed me and led me to their unmarked car. I could feel my colleagues' eyes on me as they walked past on their way into the building, and I couldn't help but feel a deep sense of shame and humiliation.

I was booked, fingerprinted, photographed, and processed. The experience was surreal and humbling; I felt like I was living someone else's life. And then, I was taken to an arraignment to see a judge.

There, I learned that I and the other four sales reps contemplating starting our own company had all been charged with fraud. The charges were severe, and I was overwhelmed by the situation's gravity. The stern and unyielding judge did not seem too pleased after a cursory review of the charges.

The charges against us were serious—allegations of forgery and fraud, which the company claimed we were responsible for. The company accused us of signing off on changes in the ad copy on behalf of our clients, a practice that had become common in our office. As ad reps, we had been trained to return ad copy to our corporate art department if there was a mistake in the ad proofs. For instance, when the art department delivered a proof for one of our advertising clients that needed corrections, like an incorrect phone number or layout, instead of taking the proof to the client, we, as the ad reps, would note the needed changes and initial the proof in our own names. This was a common practice, and we believed it a necessary and efficient way of handling minor corrections.

However, the company saw it differently and claimed our actions potentially invalidated the contract between the advertiser and the company. They accused us of engaging in fraudulent activities that undermined the business' integrity and violated our clients' trust.

The situation was complicated, and the charges against us were both puzzling and distressing. We had always acted in good faith and believed our actions aligned with the office's practices. And yet, we found ourselves facing a potentially life-altering situation that threatened to upend our careers and lives.

The charges against us were a stark reminder of the power dynamics in the corporate world and the importance of due diligence and caution in our actions.

The day of my arrest and the subsequent arraignment created a whirlwind of emotions, confusion, and disbelief. My life was being turned upside down. However, I was released immediately, with an agreement to appear at a later court date, and knew I had to take quick action.

The first step was to secure the services of an experienced attorney who could guide me through the legal process and ensure I was protected.

The plea hearing was an intense and nerve-wracking experience, and the judge insisted the prosecution and defense teams come to a reasonable agreement.

The prosecution's offer was a deal that would see me charged with a felony and ordered to repay the company the commissions I had received for the contracts I had written with advertisers where I had initialed changes to the artwork in my name. Upon repayment, or as the prosecution referred to it, "restitution," I would be eligible to have the charge reduced to a misdemeanor.

Some of my fellow sales reps had expressed a desire to fight the charges, but my attorney had warned me that would come at a high cost. The estimated cost of my defense was a staggering ten thousand dollars, without any guarantee I would win.

We felt that the charges were related to our departure plans, which made the situation all the more frustrating. We had been contemplating starting our own advertising company and were excited about our new venture's prospects. However, the company had found out about our plans and was now using the legal system to stop us.

The prospect of repaying the company a sum of eight thousand dollars was infuriating, but my attorney advised me it was the best course of action given the circumstances. He had seen similar scenarios in the corporate world before and knew the company was using the legal system to make an example of the five of us to discourage others from leaving and starting their own ventures. The goal was to send a message that the company would not tolerate such actions and would use the weight of the flawed legal system to stop anyone from leaving to compete with them.

Despite the challenges, I felt I had to take the plea deal and repay the company. It was the only way to clear my name and move on from the situation.

The sentence of restitution and probation was a harsh blow to my pride and reputation. The thought of carrying the label of a convicted felon was daunting, especially in the close-knit world of sales and advertising. The rumors of my legal troubles began to spread like wildfire, fueling speculation and damaging my credibility in the eyes of my peers and potential clients.

As I left the courthouse, I felt anger, shame, and disappointment wash over me. My once-promising future in advertising seemed to be slipping away, and the thought of facing a year of probation with the looming threat of a potential jail sentence was overwhelming.

However, my attorney assured me the terms of my probation were manageable and, with hard work, I could complete the requirements and petition the court to have the charges reduced to a misdemeanor. A monthly questionnaire and income statement, along with the requirement to make minimum payments toward restitution, court fees, and probation costs, were the only stipulations I needed to fulfill.

As I approached the probation office for my in-person appointment to set up my probation, I couldn't shake the feeling that things were not going to go as smoothly as I had hoped. The waiting area was filled with a feeling of unease, and the sounds coming from the probation officer's office only amplified my anxiety.

As I sat outside the door, I overheard a young woman inside, her sobs echoing down the hall. Although I couldn't determine the specifics of their conversation, the tone was unmistakably inappropriate and unsettling. The door opened, and the woman emerged, tears streaming down her face. The probation officer gruffly told her to have his money in his hand by the end of the week.

My heart sank as the probation officer's gaze fell on me, his eyes cold and unyielding. He gruffly told me to get into his office. As I stepped inside, I had the distinct feeling this probation officer was not to be trusted and that my time under his supervision would be fraught with difficulties and challenges.

I could feel the tension in the air when I walked into his office. It was like he was daring me to challenge his authority. The first thing he did was reach into his desk drawer and pull out a plastic cup. Slamming it on his desk, he said, "Let's go; I need a sample from you," sounding like a drill sergeant. I was taken aback, wondering what he was talking about. "A drug test," he explained, barely disguising his annoyance. I tried to show him the court order for probation did not include mandatory drug testing, but this only seemed to infuriate him further.

With a stern voice, he made it clear I was now a convict, and I better understand he was the law and had the full authority to lock me up. This was not what I had expected. He relished my discomfort while watching me provide a urine sample for the drug test.

He made it clear he would be my worst nightmare for the next year and I would have difficulty finding a decent job because no one wanted to hire a felon. He also informed me he would call my potential employers to verify I had told them of my conviction. When I mentioned my intention to pay off my restitution within two months, he scoffed and reminded me of the difficulties of being a convicted felon.

Despite my initial shame and hopelessness, I found a sales position with a company that offered business services to companies across the United States. It was a phone sales role, but I was eager for the opportunity to prove myself. I scheduled a meeting with the company's sales manager and vice president to introduce myself and explain my situation. To my relief, they were already aware of my legal troubles with my former employer and had formed their own opinions about the matter. They understood that my former employer had been excessively harsh in handling the situation and they were willing to give me a chance to prove myself. I was grateful for their understanding and determined to make the most of the opportunity.

Despite my legal troubles, I excelled in my new position, selling business services to companies across the United States over the phone. My passion for sales was reinvigorated by the opportunity to engage with business owners, learning about their unique journeys and how they got started. My success in this new role only strengthened my resolve to put the humiliating ordeal behind me as soon as possible.

And so, I set out to meet my obligations to the court, starting with the first restitution payment of nearly three thousand dollars. The amount was considerably more than the required minimum payment, but it brought me one step closer to freedom from my oppressive probation officer. I was determined to continue making larger payments until I could finally petition the court to end my probation and reduce the charges to a misdemeanor, freeing me from this chapter of my life.

Just two weeks into my new job, the probation officer made good on his threat to me by making a call to the president of my company to check if they knew they had a convicted felon on the payroll. Unfazed, the president confirmed that I'd been upfront about my legal tangles with the advertising agency and also praised my initial contributions to the company.

The next morning, my sales manager briefed me on this exchange, offering a solid vote of confidence from the company. But there was a catch. He gave me a sobering heads-up: "Watch out, that probation officer is out to make waves for you. And if he starts rocking our boat too, we might be forced to let you go." I expressed my thanks for the heads-up, yet underneath my composed exterior, I was boiling with frustration.

On Friday, I returned home after a long day at work to find my probation officer sitting in my living room, leisurely swinging one of my prized golf clubs. My heart sank as I caught a glimpse of my wife frozen in terror in the kitchen. I was filled with anger and disbelief.

"What's this all about?" I asked, trying to keep my cool.

"I received your report and saw your monthly payment was significantly larger than usual," the officer replied. "I wanted to come take a look for myself at what your home life is like."

I couldn't believe what I was hearing. Was I being accused of something? I reluctantly handed over the bank statement and paystub he demanded to see.

The officer's eyebrows rose in surprise as he scanned my pay stub. "This is more than triple what I make," he said.

I couldn't resist, my ego getting the best of me. "Yeah, that's what you can make when you have a marketable skill," I boasted, gesturing toward the golf club in his hand. "And that golf club you're holding costs more than you make in a week."

The officer looked shaken but quickly regained his composure. His response was far from what I had expected. He simply said, "Okay," and carelessly tossed my golf club in the direction of my golf bag before leaving our condo with a purposeful stride.

I couldn't help feeling a twinge of regret. How could I have been so foolish? In that moment of pride, I had let my ego get the best of me, thinking I had to push back because he meant to humiliate me in my own home and in front of my wife.

As I gazed at the discarded golf club, I realized my actions had only made things worse. Instead of backing him down, I had likely fueled his suspicion and made him even more determined to dig deeper into my life.

As soon as the door slammed shut behind him, my anger reached the boiling point. My wife stood before me, tears streaming down her face as she told me the cruel words he had spat at her. He had demanded she leave me, insisting I was a convicted criminal and a failure. He told her she deserved better—a woman as beautiful as she was should be with someone like him who could offer her needed stability. The thought of him speaking to my wife in such a manner drove me to madness.

Never in my life had I entertained the notion of taking another person's life. Not even the lives of the two boys who had tormented me as a child and left me with lasting scars. The thought of it was unsettling, yet I felt consumed by white-hot rage. I was so furious I could barely think straight. However, I knew I had to rein in my emotions. I took a deep breath and reminded myself that violence was never the answer. Instead, I would find a way to deal with this situation calmly.

I was determined not to let the probation officer ruin our weekend. We attempted to have a typical Friday, but the unpleasant experience lingered in the back of my mind. It was a constant reminder of our challenge, but I was determined to take a stand.

On Monday, I called my case manager and informed him of the ordeal I had faced with my probation officer. I wanted to make it clear I would not tolerate further mistreatment of my wife. I hoped my call would serve as a wake-up call to the probation officer to let him know that I would not roll over and let him get away with his disrespectful behavior.

As I hung up the phone, I felt empowered and relieved. I hoped my words would be heard and I could effect change for the remainder of my probation.

The following day, my workday was interrupted by an unexpected call from the probation officer himself. In a stern and threatening tone, he demanded I present myself in his office within thirty minutes or face the consequences of being "violated and sent to prison."

I tried to explain I couldn't leave work on a whim and that his office was more than thirty minutes away by car, but he was unyielding. He made it clear I had no choice and if I failed to comply, the consequences would be severe.

With a heavy heart, I went to the probation officer's office. As soon as I stepped through the door, he slammed it shut behind me, signaling the start of a tumultuous encounter. He was livid, launching into a tirade about my recent call to the case manager, his boss. He emphasized that he had all the power and he could have me thrown in prison at any moment with a single phone call to the judge.

I was taken aback by the intensity of his anger, and fear began to take hold of me as I sat in his sterile office. His aggressive demeanor and the threat of being sent to prison made me realize how dangerous this man could be. I felt powerless and at the mercy of a man who held all the cards.

When I got to work the next day, I was called to the vice president's office. I walked in, feeling uneasy and wondering what could have possibly gone wrong. The vice president said they had decided to let me go. I was stunned. I had only been there briefly and was already one of the top performers in sales.

As it turned out, the probation officer had repeatedly contacted my employer and caused a stir. Despite being fully aware of my situation before hiring me, the company was unwilling to deal with the hassle and public scrutiny the probation officer threatened to bring. I couldn't believe what I was hearing.

An overwhelming sense of helplessness washed over me once again. I felt like the ground had been pulled out from under me, and I was spiraling out of control. For the next two months, I went on countless job interviews, pouring my heart out to potential employers about my legal troubles. But no matter how candid I was, no one offered me a job.

As the days passed, our savings dwindled at an alarming rate. I was forced to make only the minimum payments toward my restitution.

The thought of losing my ability to quickly pay off my debt and put this whole ordeal behind me was a constant source of despair.

The ordeal was taking a toll on me. I felt like a loser, as less of a man. I couldn't even provide for my family. Staving off depression felt like swimming upstream in quicksand. My wife started talking about separating, and I fought to keep myself together; I mean, who could blame her? She didn't sign up for this.

One day, I got a call from a construction supply company based in Phoenix, about two hours away. It was looking to expand into the Tucson area. I spoke with the district manager by phone. I told him about my legal challenges and what he might have to deal with from my probation officer. He said he, too, had dealt with an aggressive probation officer and he'd have no issues telling mine to back off. I was elated; we agreed I would drive to Phoenix to meet in person later that week.

On the day of the meeting, I hopped on my motorcycle to make the two-hour drive to Phoenix. On the way out of town, I stopped at an ATM to pull out money to fill up my gas tank. It was humiliating to go inside the bank because I had less than twenty dollars in my account. I withdrew sixteen dollars. As I was sheepishly waiting for the teller to count out the ten, the five, and the one-dollar bill, I noticed a cart at the next teller where they were pulling the cash from the drawer. There must have been thousands of dollars in cash just sitting there. Me, a couple of tellers, and a bank manager who had just walked into a back office were alone in the bank. My heart sank as I remembered a time, not long before, when I would not have even noticed the thousands of dollars in cash just sitting there. Anger about my situation boiled within me.

Just as I was about to hop on my bike, my phone chimed to life. It was my probation officer on the line, and I couldn't help but feel a twinge of annoyance. At twenty-five years old, the idea of answering to a probation officer felt more than a little frustrating. Part of me wanted to ignore the call, but I took a deep breath, found my inner calm, and answered the phone.

"What are you doing?" he asked.

"I'm on my way to an interview for a job."

He laughed and said, "Why bother? You're not going to get hired with me in their ear! Who are you interviewing with?"

I told him about the company and the position.

"Wait, the company is in Phoenix? Are you going there for the interview?"

Of course, I was going there; that's where the company was. Did he somehow know this already? Was that why he called in the first place?

"You can't leave the county without my permission," he said smugly.

My heart sank. Then he said, "And I'm not granting permission."

I fought to keep my cool, reminding myself I had only five more months of probation, according to the terms of the plea agreement.

What he said next wholly overtook my ability to see a way out.

"By the way, I'm petitioning the court to extend your probationary period by another twelve months, citing your inability to find work and complete your restitution within the current timeframe of the plea agreement." He laughed maniacally as I hung up on him.

I called the company to cancel my interview, explaining the situation to the manager. He sympathized with my frustration and reminded me that the probation officer wielded nearly unchecked control over me and would continue to be a menace until I could pay the rest of the restitution and petition the court.

Dark thoughts and plots ran through my mind as I returned home. The look of disappointment and frustration from my wife only deepened my shame. I needed to do something fast. I took a paper route to get some cash, though I knew it would not be enough. And the stop, start, and mileage was tough on the only car we had left between us. We'd sold mine to pay bills and restitution for the previous two months.

The probation officer made good on his threat, and the court extended my probation another twelve months. I could not endure another year of this man ruining my life. I suddenly remembered an article I'd read in a national men's magazine in the waiting room of a doctor's office. It was about a pair of bank robbers the FBI had assigned one of their most famous profilers to hunt down.

Time seemed to stand still as I recalled the details about how they'd gotten away with more than thirty bank robberies throughout the eastern United States. The FBI profiler interviewed said they were so challenging to capture because they were in and out of the banks quickly, before the dispatch call could even go out over the airwaves.

I began thinking about all the cash sitting on the cart at the bank where I'd withdrawn sixteen of my last twenty dollars. As I thought about other ways to get quick cash, I couldn't get past the awful things I'd have to do. I didn't want to get mixed up in selling drugs, and I didn't want to rob anyone, steal cars, or do anything else that would directly hurt anyone.

As I continued thinking about that article, I convinced myself that robbing a bank was a victimless crime. I wouldn't be taking money from anyone personally...what was the harm? I reflected on my situation and the injustice of the legal system and its officers. My probation officer constantly reminded me he was an officer of the court. The more I thought about all of this, the more convinced I became that bank robbery would be the solution to a problem I could not see going away anytime soon.

I felt desperate, and I hated feeling that way. I weighed the advantages of robbery with the fact that it was morally wrong and that even if I were never caught, I would have to live with the guilt of my action and never tell a soul about it for the rest of my life. On the other hand, my life felt like it was falling apart already. I was broke, I couldn't get a job making any reasonable income, my wife was about to leave me, and I imagined the shame and humiliation I would feel for not being man enough to do what was needed to provide for my family.

It is incredible how the mind can quickly justify a course of action under duress. Later, this concept would become something I became obsessed with studying.

## The Power of Circumstances

The power of circumstances can be immense. The situations we find ourselves in can dictate much of our lives, from the opportunities we have to the choices we make. Sometimes, our circumstances can feel insurmountable, leaving us feeling trapped and helpless.

Recognizing the power of circumstances is essential, but it is also important not to give up control of them. While we may not always be able to control the situation we find ourselves in, we can always control how we respond. It is up to us to decide how to navigate the obstacles life throws our way.

The consequences ofbeing trapped by circumstances can be devastating. When we allow our circumstances to dictate our lives, we give up our agency and ability to shape our future. We may find ourselves stuck in a cycle of negative thinking, feeling as though we are powerless to change our situation. This can lead to depression, anxiety, and hopelessness.

I know this all too well from my experience in the grip of circumstance. I was trapped in a cycle of poverty, heartbreak, and legal troubles, feeling like I had no way out. My circumstances had shaped much of my life, and I felt powerless to change them. Only when I realized I had the power to take control of my own life was I able to break free from my circumstance.

The lesson from my experience is that it is possible to take charge of life, no matter how dire the circumstances may seem. While events may shape our lives, they do not have to define them. Here are some steps for breaking free from the grip of circumstance:

1. **Take responsibility for your life.**

   The first step in taking charge of your life is taking responsibility for it. Recognize that you are the only one who can control your actions and your reactions to the circumstances you face. It is up to you to decide how to respond to the challenges life throws your way.

2. **Reframe your thinking.**

   How we think about our circumstances can significantly influence how we feel. Our feelings and behavior can help us break free from negative thought patterns and open up new possibilities. Rather than seeing our circumstances as limitations, we can see them as opportunities for growth and change.

3. **Set goals.**

   Setting goals can help us focus our energy and efforts on what we want to achieve. By setting specific, achievable goals, we can create a roadmap for our lives that can help us break free from the grip of circumstance. It is essential to set realistic and achievable goals that also push us outside of our comfort zones.

4. **Take action.**

   Action is the key to breaking free from the grip of circumstance. It is not enough to set goals and hope things will change. We must take deliberate, focused action to move toward our goals and create the life we want.

5. **Practice self-care.**

   Taking charge of our lives can be complex and challenging, but caring for ourselves is essential. This means practicing self-care and making time for the things that bring us joy and fulfillment. Caring for ourselves can build the resilience and strength needed to navigate life's challenges.

### Recognizing the Grip of Circumstance

In my experience, recognizing the grip of circumstance is the first step in taking charge of your life. Circumstances can be both external and internal and affect your life in various ways. External circumstances include financial struggles, complex relationships, health issues, and other external factors beyond your control. Internal circumstances include limiting beliefs, self-doubt, and negative self-talk. Regardless of their nature, these circumstances can make you feel trapped and like you have no control over your life.

The first step in recognizing the grip of circumstance is to acknowledge you're experiencing it. It's important to understand that feeling like a victim of circumstances is not uncommon and is not a sign of weakness. However, realizing you can change your circumstances is crucial, even if it initially seems impossible.

### The Role of Mindset in Determining Outcomes

Your mindset plays a crucial role in determining your outcomes. The way you think about yourself and your circumstances can influence your behavior and the actions you take. If you have a negative mindset, you're more likely to feel like a victim of circumstance and believe you have no control over your life.

On the other hand, if you have a positive mindset, you're more likely to believe you can take control and change your circumstances. Having a positive mindset doesn't mean you're in denial of your problems or ignoring your situation's reality. Instead, it means you're focusing on what you can control and taking action to improve your life.

### The Dangers of a Victim Mentality

The victim mentality is a dangerous mindset that can prevent you from taking charge of your life. It's characterized by a sense of helplessness and a belief that you have no control over your circumstances. When you have a victim mentality, you're more likely to blame external factors for your problems and feel like you're not responsible.

The victim mentality can be a self-fulfilling prophecy because it can prevent you from taking action and changing your life. When you believe you're a victim of circumstances, you're less likely to take responsibility for your life and work to improve your situation.

### Identifying Limiting Beliefs and Negative Self-Talk

Limiting beliefs and negative self-talk can contribute to the grip of circumstances and prevent you from taking charge of your life. Limiting beliefs are beliefs that hold you back and prevent you from achieving your goals. Negative self-talk is the inner voice that tells you that you're not good enough, smart enough, or capable enough to succeed.

Identifying limiting beliefs and negative self-talk is the first step in overcoming them. Challenging these beliefs and replacing them with more empowering thoughts is essential. For example, if you believe you're not good enough to succeed, challenge that belief by reminding yourself of your accomplishments and what you're good at.

Taking charge of your life and breaking free from circumstance requires a mindset shift and a commitment to action. Recognizing the grip of circumstance, adopting a positive mindset, avoiding a victim mentality, and identifying limiting beliefs and negative self-talk are all essential steps in taking charge of your life. Remember, you can change your circumstances and take control of your life. Don't let external or internal circumstances prevent you from achieving your goals and living your desired life.

### Understanding the Power of Choice

Life is an infinite series of choices. Each decision we make shapes the trajectory of our lives. However, when we feel trapped by circumstance, we quickly forget that we have the power to choose. It is essential to understand that our choices are the driving force behind our lives, and taking ownership of them is crucial in breaking free from the grip of circumstance.

### Taking Responsibility for Our Choices

We must recognize that our choices have consequences. Every decision can take us one step closer to or farther away from our goals. We must take responsibility for our choices and be accountable for their outcomes. When we accept responsibility for our choices, we gain the power to make different choices and change our lives.

## The Importance of Embracing the Power of Choice

The power of choice is an incredible gift we all have. However, many of us take this gift for granted. We must embrace the power of choice and use it to our advantage. When we make deliberate choices, we gain control over our lives. Then we can start to shape the future into what we want for ourselves. We must always appreciate the power of our choices and their effect on our lives.

## Overcoming Fear and Uncertainty to Make Bold Choices

Fear and uncertainty are the two biggest obstacles to making bold choices. Fear of failure, fear of the unknown, and fear of change can paralyze us, making it difficult to make choices that will help us break free from the grip of circumstance. However, we must recognize that fear and uncertainty are natural and part of growth. We must learn to embrace our fears, acknowledge them, and move forward with courage, despite the uncertainty. By making bold choices, we can break the grip of circumstance and unleash our full potential.

Taking charge of your life is about recognizing the power of choice and taking ownership of your preferences. When you understand the effect of your choices, you gain control over your life and can start to shape the future you want for yourself. To make bold choices, it is essential to embrace the power of choice, take responsibility for your choices, and overcome fear and uncertainty. By doing so, you can break free from the grip of circumstance and unleash your full potential. Remember, your life is your own; you can shape it however you choose.

## Taking Action to Break Free from Circumstances

Taking charge of your life is not easy, but it's one of the most important things you can do. If you're feeling stuck or trapped by circumstances, the first step to breaking free is to recognize you have the power to change your situation. Below, I discuss how to break free from circumstances, recognize the need for change, set goals, take action, and overcome setbacks and obstacles.

## Recognizing the Need for Change

The first step to breaking free from circumstances is recognizing the need for change. This is not always easy, but it's necessary if you want to move forward. It's easy to fall into the trap of feeling like things are out of your control and you can't do anything to change your situation. However, the truth is you have the power to change your life. That starts by acknowledging something needs to change.

## The Importance of Setting Goals and Taking Action

Once you've recognized the need for change, the next step is to set goals and act. Setting goals is essential because it gives you something to work toward. It helps you focus your energy and effort on something positive. Without goals, it's easy to feel lost and directionless. Once you've set your goals, it's essential to act. You can have the best goals in the world, but they're only meaningful if you take the action needed to achieve them. Acting requires courage and determination, but it's the only way to progress.

## Overcoming Setbacks and Obstacles

Taking action to break free from circumstances can be challenging. You will face setbacks and obstacles along the way, but it's important to avoid letting them derail you. It's easy to get discouraged and feel like giving up when things don't go as planned. However, setbacks and obstacles are a normal part of the process. Learning from them, adapting, and moving forward is essential.

## The Power of Perseverance

Breaking free from circumstances requires perseverance. Change can be challenging and is rarely a quick fix so it's essential to keep pushing forward, even when things get tough. The power of perseverance separates those who succeed from those who give up. It allows you to keep going when everything seems to be against you.

Taking charge of your life is recognizing you can change your circumstances. It requires setting goals, taking action, and persevering through setbacks and obstacles. It's not always easy, but it's worth it. When you take charge of your life, you give yourself the power to create the life you want. Don't let circumstances hold you back. Embrace the power of choice, and act to break free from the grip of circumstances.

## The Power of Taking Charge of Your Life

As I reflect on my personal experience with the grip of circumstance, I can't help but recognize the power of taking charge of my life. It is easy to fall into the trap of feeling like our lives are out of our control and we are at the mercy of our circumstances. However, the truth is we have more power than we realize.

One of the most significant lessons I learned from my experience is we always have a choice. We can choose to stay trapped in our circumstances or take action to change them. We can choose to focus on things outside our control or take ownership of our lives and take steps to move forward.

### The Benefits of Breaking Free from Circumstances

Breaking free from the grip of circumstances can be challenging, but the benefits are significant. When we take charge of our lives, we create a sense of empowerment and control that can transform our lives. We feel more confident, capable, and in control of our future.

Breaking free from circumstances also allows us to pursue our goals and dreams. When circumstances no longer limit us, we can take risks, try new things, and push ourselves to reach our full potential. This, in turn, leads to a more fulfilling and satisfying life.

### Final Words of Encouragement and Advice

If you find yourself trapped in the grip of circumstance, I encourage you to take action to break free. Recognize you can take charge of your life and make changes that will lead to a better future.

Start by identifying the areas where you feel stuck and begin to take steps to move forward in them. Set clear goals, break them down into smaller steps, and act consistently. Don't let setbacks or obstacles discourage you; instead, see them as an opportunity to learn and grow.

Finally, don't be afraid to seek support from others. Surround yourself with people who believe in you, encourage you, and challenge you to be your best self. With the right mindset, support, and actions, you can break free from the grip of circumstance and create a fulfilling, satisfying life that aligns with your dreams.

## Self-Reflection

The real progress to be found in this material is when you take the time to reflect on the questions presented in the chapter. Writing out your answers will provoke pattern changes when you face adversity in the future, providing access to new tools and ways of facing adversity. Take advantage of the opportunity to truly unleash your potential!

## Questions to Reflect On

- Which limiting beliefs have held you back in the past, and how can you challenge them to break free from the grip of circumstance?
- What small steps can you take to start taking control of your life and shape the future you want for yourself?
- How can you overcome fear and uncertainty to make bold choices that will help you break free from the grip of circumstance?
- Which goal have you been putting off because you feel trapped by circumstance, and what action can you take today to start working toward it?

## Summary

- Recognize the power of circumstances and their influence on your life, but don't let them control you.
- Take responsibility for your life and choices, even when faced with difficult circumstances.
- Reframe your thinking to see circumstances as opportunities for growth and change, not just limitations.
- Set specific, achievable goals to create a roadmap for your life and focus your efforts.
- Take deliberate, focused action to move toward your goals and create the life you want for yourself.
- Practice self-care and make time for things that bring you joy and fulfillment to build resilience and strength.
- Adopt a positive mindset to believe you can control your life and change your circumstances.
- Identify limiting beliefs and negative self-talk that hold you back and challenge them, replacing them with more empowering thoughts.

## Conclusion

This chapter explored the power of circumstances and their effect on our lives. You learned that taking charge of your life involves taking responsibility for your actions, embracing the power of choice, setting goals, taking action, and persevering through setbacks and obstacles. Doing so allows you to break free from circumstances and unlock your full potential. Taking charge of your life is not easy, but it's worth it.

You have the power to create the life you want to live, and with the right mindset, support, and actions, you can achieve your dreams.

# UNLEASHING YOUR OWN POTENTIAL

with Robert Henry

# 4

# FORGETTING YOUR VALUES: THE SLIPPERY SLOPE OF COMPROMISING YOUR INTEGRITY

*"Adversity introduces a man to himself."*

— Albert Einstein

I decided I was going to do it. I'd rob a bank. I'd take the cash to another bank a few days later and purchase a cashier's check in the amount of my remaining restitution. I would immediately petition the court to be released from probation and the grips of the tyrannical probation officer. It felt like a lifeline.

I even entertained thoughts of somehow anonymously returning the bank's money at some point in the future after I got my life back on track.

My heart raced for days as I planned my approach. I thought about all the things that would enable a quick getaway. I bought a radio and researched the trunking codes for local law enforcement radio dispatch so I could, with an earpiece, hear the police dispatch calls in real-time. I thought about how to effectively, but subtly, disguise my appearance, not so much that it would be evident to observers as I entered the bank, but enough to make it difficult to identify me as the robber if it were to air on television or be printed in newspapers.

I felt a bit of exhilaration while planning the heist. Sure, I was scared, nervous, and worried about getting caught, but it felt like I was taking back control of my life, which felt good. I was done being timid, weak, and controlled by this evil man.

As I made my way through Tucson's quiet, deserted streets, the sky was cast in a dark, ominous gray hue, with raindrops pitter-pattering against the pavement. I was in disguise, my earpiece and radio in place, and I tightly gripped a faux pistol resembling a Glock.

I had done extensive research and learned tellers were trained to hand over the cash without hesitation in a bank robbery. But despite my meticulous preparation, I couldn't shake the fear that gnawed at the pit of my stomach.

I had never held a real pistol, let alone used one to rob a bank. The thought of accidentally shooting myself, or worse, an innocent bystander, filled me with dread and terror. But what if the teller realized my gun was fake?

As I pushed open the bank doors, my heart racing with fear and adrenaline, a thought suddenly struck me like a bolt of lightning. I had been so focused on my action plan that I had failed to consider the possibility of an armed guard standing inside.

Stepping cautiously into the bank, I scanned the room with heightened awareness, searching for any signs of danger. To my immense relief, there was no sign of an armed guard, and the few people in the bank were engrossed in their own business, paying me no mind.

I made my way to the back of the line where a handful of people were waiting. Only when I reached the front of the line and faced the teller across the counter did the absurdity of the situation fully dawn on me. Here I was following the conventions of polite society by waiting in line when I was there to rob the institution.

My heart pounded in my chest, and the entire scene felt like a dream—an improbable and surreal moment. The voice of reason whispered in my ear, urging me to back out and leave this foolish endeavor behind. But it was too late for second thoughts. I had come too far.

The teller at the far end of the counter beckoned me, her demeanor impatient and businesslike. She appeared to be a woman on the cusp of retirement, with a face etched with lines of experience and a no-nonsense attitude. I couldn't help wondering if she had some sort of premonition of my true intentions.

Time seemed to slow to a crawl as I stood before her, frozen in indecision. When she repeated her question, "Sir, can I help you?" I was jolted back to reality.

I attempted to put on a gruff exterior, adopting the persona of a seasoned bank robber, as I issued my demands. "You can put your twenties, fifties, and hundreds on the counter right now," I said, my voice shaking with a mixture of fear and adrenaline.

The teller's expression didn't change; she simply regarded me blankly as if she had seen it all before. Then, sounding annoyed, she replied, "I'm sorry; what can I help you with?"

I was taken aback by her nonchalant attitude. I struggled to understand how she could be indifferent to the situation. Was she hard of hearing? I was trying to cause as little commotion as possible, but her lack of urgency and understanding was beginning to rattle me.

Determined to make my intentions clear, I lifted up my shirt slightly to expose the fake gun tucked into my waistband. I sternly repeated my demand for the twenties, fifties, and hundreds, hoping to convey the gravity of the situation.

With an almost imperceptible eyeroll and a deep sigh of annoyance, the teller began placing a few five- and ten-dollar bills on the counter at a painfully slow pace. I couldn't believe what was happening. This woman was completely unfazed by me or the situation at hand, and her lack of urgency jeopardized my plan.

Panic started to set in as I realized I had to do something drastic and fast. I had been monitoring the police dispatch radio traffic through one earpiece, but what if I had missed something crucial? What if the police were already on their way? My goal had been to be in and out of the bank within ninety seconds, but this teller was making that impossible.

As the moments ticked by, my anxiety grew. Had I programmed in all of the trunking codes? Was I missing important updates on the police's movements? The pressure was mounting, and I knew I needed to move before it was too late.

Desperate to move things along, I withdrew the fake pistol from my waistband and placed it as menacingly as possible on the counter. This seemed to get the teller's attention, and a few twenties and fifties began appearing. However, my nerves were fraying as I noticed that other tellers were observing the tense interaction at the end of their counter. Their curious gazes only added to my anxiety, and I became more frantic in my attempts to speed things along.

The sound of shuffling money and the teller's slow movements filled the air, contrasting my rapidly beating heart and racing thoughts. I was acutely aware that every second that passed increased the chances of someone calling the police or doing something to foil my plans. The pressure was mounting, and I felt like I was in a spiraling vortex of pressure, like the walls were closing in.

Finally, I mustered up the courage to speak, instructing her to place her hands on the counter and not say a word until two minutes after I left the bank. The teller was not intimidated by me or my fake weapon; instead, she gazed at me with a disapproving thousand-yard stare that seemed to look straight into my soul. I felt she was silently judging me for my actions.

With shaking hands, I quickly gathered all the bills and crammed them into a nearby merchant zip-up bag. My pulse was pounding in my ears, and I couldn't help feeling a rising panic that everything was going wrong. I was acutely aware time was of the essence. I had to get out of the bank as soon as possible.

As I left the bank, my heart was pounding so hard I could feel it in my throat. I felt a mix of excitement, fear, and disbelief that I had done it! I had accomplished something I had been planning for weeks, but I couldn't shake the nagging feeling that something might go wrong.

As I made my way through the parking lot, relief over my success was quickly replaced with panic as a car nosed into the parking space beside me. A police car with two officers inside was pulling into the bank parking lot! My heart skipped a beat as I wondered if they were there for me.

When the officer in the driver's seat glanced in my direction, my heart sank. Had they received a call? Were they about to draw their guns on me? I struggled to maintain my composure as my mind raced with possibilities. My mind searched for any possible explanation for why the police were there.

As I tried to act nonchalant and continued walking toward my motorcycle parked around the corner, I couldn't shake the feeling I was being watched. Every step felt like an eternity as I waited for something to happen. Finally, I turned the corner and broke into a run, knowing I had to put as much distance as possible between the bank and me.

As I straddled my motorcycle, I couldn't help but feel excitement and adrenaline. The thrill of the chase was already starting to course through my veins when I heard the crackle of the police radio dispatch. It was the call I had expected, but listening to it and the dispatcher describing the robber close to my appearance and the bank I'd just exited was surreal!

As I gunned the engine and pulled away from the bank, I tried to stay calm, but my hands were shaking on the handlebars. I couldn't believe I had been so close to getting caught!

I weaved through traffic, trying to stay inconspicuous, but every siren and flashing light felt like the police were closing in on me. It was a race against time, and I had to get out of the area as quickly as possible. I could hear the screeching of tires and the blaring of police sirens coming from the opposite direction, and my heart felt like it was going to beat out of my chest.

Finally, I saw an opening in traffic and took the chance to gun it. I accelerated as fast as possible, leaving the scene far behind me. The wind rushed past me as I rode away, and I couldn't help but feel a sense of exhilaration and fear all at once.

Later, as I tallied the cash I had taken—a modest $2,400—a wave of relief washed over me. It could cover a few bills and chip away at the restitution I owed. Yet, as I examined those numbers, it became evident it wouldn't be sufficient. The urgency for more money became glaringly apparent. I needed it, and I needed it quickly. Desperate, I knew what I had to do. I had to rob another bank and ensure I got a better haul. It was a risky move, but I had no other options. I scoured the area, looking for the perfect target.

I found a nearby bank that looked just as vulnerable as the last one. I began to scope it out, studying its layout, security cameras, and traffic patterns. It was all starting to feel familiar, and I couldn't help but wonder if I was getting in over my head.

However, the thought of what I could do with the money was too tempting to ignore. I could finally pay off all my debts and start fresh. It was a chance to create a new life free of the burdens that had been weighing me down.

With a mix of fear and excitement, I started planning the next robbery. I studied the bank's security measures, planned my escape route, and ensured my equipment was in order. I knew the risks, but I also knew I had come too far to turn back.

The night before the heist, I barely slept. My mind was racing with a million different scenarios, each more terrifying than the last. I knew the stakes were high, and the slightest mistake could mean disaster. But I also knew I had to go through with it.

The next day, I put my plan into action. I moved calmly, knowing I had prepared for every possible contingency. I was in and out of the bank in minutes with a haul far exceeding my expectations, this time more than twenty-thousand dollars. As I made my escape, I could feel the rush of adrenaline once again coursing through my veins.

After the second bank, I had enough to get a cashier's check to pay off my restitution in full. It was a massive weight off my shoulders since I could then petition the court to release me from probation and reduce the charge hanging over my head. I longed for freedom from the suffocating grasp of my probation officer, who had been making my life a nightmare.

To my relief, the court agreed to set aside the reporting requirements that were part of my probation. I was no longer required to report to my probation officer regularly, which felt like a breath of fresh air. However, it came with a catch. I would remain in a probationary status until the end of my probation term, which was another fourteen long months. That meant I needed to continue adhering to the terms of my probation and stay on my best behavior to avoid further legal entanglements.

While this situation was better than nothing, I had hoped for a different outcome. It meant for the next fourteen months I still had to disclose my conviction at job interviews, which would inevitably create obstacles.

Looking back, I can't help wondering what could have been if I had made different choices. A brighter, more level-headed version of me would have resumed my job search or taken on several jobs to make ends meet, riding out the remainder of my probation. But something inside me couldn't bear the thought of continuing to struggle that way.

Now, the guilt of being a criminal and living out my days as an outlaw weighed heavily on my mind.

I let my wife believe I was working for the construction supply company based in Phoenix. But that was far from true. I continued robbing banks. Several in Tucson and more in Phoenix. It was a dangerous and reckless path, but it seemed like my only option.

Remember, the thoughts we entertain tremendously influence our actions and decisions. By becoming aware of our internal dialogue and using techniques like challenging limiting beliefs and visualization, we can take control of our thinking and move toward a more fulfilling and authentic life. Had I challenged my limiting beliefs rather than let them control my vision of the future, I might have made a better future for myself.

## Cultivating Resilience to Adversity

It's easy to convince ourselves our actions are justified, especially when facing adversity. However, it's essential to understand our choices under stress can change our lives forever. That's why it's crucial to build resilience to adversity and learn strategies for overcoming challenges and setbacks.

Resilience is the ability to recover quickly from difficulties and setbacks. It's a crucial skill to develop because life is full of challenges and setbacks are inevitable. When we face adversity, it's easy to feel overwhelmed and powerless; therefore, focusing on what we can control is essential.

Developing a growth mindset is one of the best ways to build resilience. With a growth mindset, we believe our abilities and intelligence can be developed over time. Then we're more likely to see challenges as opportunities for growth and setbacks as temporary obstacles to overcome.

Another important strategy for building resilience is to cultivate a robust support system. Surrounding ourselves with people who offer emotional support and encouragement can make a significant difference in our ability to recover from setbacks. Whether they are friends, family, or a professional support network, having people we can rely on will help us navigate difficult times and emerge stronger.

Remembering we're not alone in facing adversity is essential. Many successful people have faced setbacks and failures before achieving their goals. Setbacks can be valuable opportunities to learn and grow, leading us to discover new paths and opportunities we may not have considered otherwise.

Ultimately, building resilience is about learning to adapt to change and developing the skills and mindset necessary to overcome challenges. By focusing on what we can control, adopting a growth mindset, and cultivating a robust support system, we can navigate challenging times more easily and emerge stronger on the other side.

## Cultivating Self-Awareness

Self-awareness is a critical component of personal growth and success. By being in tune with our values and beliefs, we can make decisions that align with who we are and what we stand for. When we compromise our values, we lose our integrity and hinder our progress.

Developing self-awareness is not always easy, but it is necessary. We must take the time to reflect on our thoughts, feelings, and behavior and be honest with ourselves about what we find. This process may be challenging, but the benefits will be immense.

By being true to ourselves, we can build more meaningful relationships with others and find greater fulfillment in our lives. When we are honest with ourselves, we can set better goals, make better decisions, and live a more fulfilling life. Self-reflection is a critical tool in this process. By reflecting on our experiences, we can gain new insights and perspectives that can help us grow and develop.

Strategies for developing self-awareness include meditation, journaling, talking to a trusted friend or mentor, and seeking feedback from others. By engaging in these activities, we can develop a deeper understanding of ourselves and our values and make better decisions in the face of adversity.

Remember, it is essential to cultivate self-awareness; knowing who we are makes being true to ourselves possible and can lead to a more fulfilling life. When we are honest with ourselves, we can make better decisions and achieve our goals with integrity and purpose.

## Choosing to Live with Integrity

Living with integrity means aligning our actions with our values and holding ourselves accountable for our decisions. Having integrity is not always easy; it often requires making difficult choices that may not be popular or convenient. However, the benefits of living with integrity are immeasurable. When we choose to live with integrity, we gain self-respect and self-worth, allowing us to build strong relationships with others based on mutual trust and respect.

Having integrity also positively influences our mental health and well-being. When we are true to ourselves and our values, we experience a sense of inner peace and contentment that cannot be found through external means. We become more resilient to life's challenges because we have a strong foundation of self-awareness and purpose to guide us.

To live with integrity, we must be willing to examine our beliefs and values and be honest with ourselves about our strengths and weaknesses. We must also be willing to take ownership of our decisions, even when it's difficult, and learn from our mistakes. This ownership requires a willingness to be vulnerable, open to feedback, and committed to ongoing personal growth and development.

Ultimately, the choice to live with integrity means prioritizing our well-being and that of others over short-term gain or convenience. It's choosing to lead a meaningful, purposeful, and fulfilling life, and to make a positive difference in the world around us. Living with integrity sets us up for a life of happiness, fulfillment, and success.

When we understand the dangers of compromising our integrity and how to build resilience to adversity, we can learn to make better decisions under stress and pressure. Cultivating self-awareness and understanding the power of our thoughts can help us live with integrity, even in challenging circumstances. Then we can build a life aligned with our values and experience greater fulfillment and success.

## Self-Reflection

Please take a few moments to reflect on the questions below. They are designed to provoke pattern changes when you face adversity in the future, providing you with new tools and ways to develop integrity and be guided by it when facing adversity. Remember, the real value of this material is reflecting on how you can apply these lessons to your own life when you write out the answers to the questions.

## Questions to Reflect On

- When was the last time you compromised your values, and how did that compromise affect your life?
- How can you cultivate self-awareness to understand your values and beliefs better and live with integrity?
- What strategies can you use to control negative self-talk and build resilience when facing adversity in the future?
- How can you build a strong support system to help you remain accountable and maintain your integrity when facing difficult situations?

- What techniques can you use to visualize yourself living with integrity, and how can they help you make better decisions when faced with challenging circumstances?
- What actions can you take today to align your actions with your values and live a life of integrity, even when it is difficult to do so?

**Summary**

- Be clear about your values and beliefs, and make a conscious effort to live in alignment with them.
- Develop self-awareness to recognize when your actions are not in line with your values and take steps to address them.
- Avoid rationalizing unethical behavior by reminding yourself of your values and the long-term consequences of compromising them.
- Practice resilience-building techniques to help overcome adversity and stay true to your values in challenging situations.
- Use visualization techniques to see yourself acting in accordance with your values and beliefs.
- Surround yourself with a robust support system that holds you accountable to your values and helps you stay on track.
- Choose to live with integrity by holding yourself to high ethical standards, even when it's difficult or unpopular.

- Remember that living with integrity benefits you, those around you, and the world.

## Conclusion

I trust you have gained a new perspective on the power of values and beliefs, the importance of staying true to yourself, and the significant influence that living with integrity can have on your life. Remember, our thoughts influence our actions, and building resilience to adversity is crucial in overcoming challenges and setbacks.

Cultivating self-awareness, living with integrity, and being accountable for your actions will help you avoid the slippery slope of compromising your integrity and provide you with the tools and mindset needed to tackle future obstacles. I challenge you to take a moment to reflect on your values; consider how they have guided your past actions and how you can continue to use them to shape your future. Remember, you have the power to live a life of integrity. I encourage you to take the steps necessary to make that a reality.

# UNLEASHING YOUR OWN POTENTIAL

with Robert Henry

# 5

# FACING THE CONSEQUENCES: TAKING OWNERSHIP OF YOUR DECISIONS

*"I am not what happened to me; I am what I choose to become."*

— Carl Jung

I had reached a breaking point, worn down by the constant risks and the exhausting double life I led as a secret criminal. The guilt of deceiving my wife and the relentless anxiety every time a police car loomed in my rearview mirror had become unbearable.

In my quest for an escape, I devised a plan to rob a series of banks in quick succession, aiming to gather enough money to buy a van and a carpet cleaning machine. Leveraging my experience in advertising and my strong work ethic, I believed I could create a legitimate business, complete with a loyal customer base, and secure a decent living. The idea resonated deeply within me.

Having already pulled off numerous bank heists in Tucson and Phoenix, I knew it was unwise to continue in my immediate surroundings. So, I embarked on a journey to San Diego, where I intended to execute a string of bank robberies in just a matter of days.

Upon arrival in San Diego, I checked into a hotel and started scouting potential banks. I favored locations within bustling shopping centers, complete with grocery stores and a strip of shops. The ideal bank was close to a highway, ideally near a highway interchange, to obscure any potential escape routes.

My search led me to a Bank of America that met all the criteria—it was perfect. Because a recent thunderstorm had passed through, the late afternoon light was dim and traffic was sparse. *This would have been the perfect time to rob this bank*, I couldn't help thinking.

Eager to get the job done and, perhaps recklessly, skipping my usual preparations, I decided on the spot to rob the bank. Walking in, even though it had become somewhat routine, I still felt a surge of adrenaline as I confronted two tellers.

Stepping out of the bank, I hopped onto the highway, the distant sound of sirens approaching the scene. With a sense of confidence in my successful getaway, I made my way back to the hotel.

After counting the money, I decided to eat a nice meal at the hotel's steakhouse. As I showered and changed into my dinner clothes, I felt a twinge of nervousness in my gut. I had never been a fan of sticking around after a job, but something about this hotel and its location made me feel safe.

While still in my room getting ready, I checked the weather outside and noticed that the I-8 freeway had been shut down in both directions. *Must be a big accident*, I thought. But as I peered closer, I realized the police activity surrounding the freeway and the row of hotels was intense. I had never seen so many police cars before, which made me uneasy.

Despite my uneasiness, I decided to continue with my plan to enjoy a celebratory meal. I left my room and started down the hall toward the elevator. I soon realized my mistake when I heard police radios blaring on my floor. The officers were exiting the elevator, and their radios were broadcasting the description of a bank robber. My heart started racing—I knew I was in trouble.

I had made a grave error by staying at the hotel. The police were closing in on me, and I had nowhere to run. I was trapped, with no choice but to face the consequences of my actions.

My heart was pounding as I sprinted back to my hotel room. I knew I had to act fast if I wanted to avoid getting caught. As I entered my room, I frantically wiped down the merchant bag that contained the stolen money. I knew I needed to get rid of it before it attracted unwanted attention.

I quickly decided to leave my room to hide the money. I headed toward the bank of elevators on the other side of the hotel. I knew I had to stay calm and collected, but my heart pounded as I walked through the halls. My palms were sweating, and I was afraid I would attract attention from the police officers undoubtedly scouring the area for the bank robber.

As I approached the bank of elevators, I spotted a vending machine and quickly ducked behind it. The adrenaline coursed through my veins. My hands shook as I placed the bag behind the machine. I took a deep breath and tried to calm down.

Once I had ditched the bag, I realized I needed to leave the hotel quickly. I contemplated returning to my room, but I knew it was too risky. I assumed the police were already on their way there, and I couldn't afford to get caught. As I turned to leave, I heard the unmistakable sound of footsteps coming down the hall toward me. I had to move fast.

I headed to the other set of elevators to put some distance between myself and the police. As I made my way to the lobby, I felt like I was in a spy movie. Every step I took was fraught with danger. I had to stay calm and collected to leave the hotel undetected.

My adrenaline was pumping as I tried to make my way out, but my escape was foiled by a group of officers standing in my path, waiting to enter the elevator. I kept my cool, nodding at them as I walked right through the middle of the group and made my way through the lobby toward the exit. I was sure they would catch me at any moment.

As I approached the door, an officer stepped in front of me, blocking my way. I said, "Good evening," and casually moved to go past him. He stopped me and explained that no one could leave the hotel because they were searching for a fugitive. My mind raced as I tried to come up with a plan. I couldn't return to my room, but I couldn't stay here either. I was trapped.

Thinking quickly on my feet, I made my way to a nearby restaurant, praying that I could seamlessly blend in among the other diners. I did my best to appear nonchalant, ordering a meal and hoping to outlast the search effort. While taking my seat, the police radios crackled with my description: "Suspect is a white male, in his mid to late twenties, standing at six feet with blonde hair and a goatee." I stood at six-foot-two with hair that fell somewhere between blonde and brown. Holding my breath, I hoped these small discrepancies would be enough to keep me incognito. Just as I began to relax, a pair of officers entered the restaurant, scanning the room. My heart leaped into my throat as they headed toward my table. I could feel their eyes on me. I tried to act natural, pretending to read the menu.

They gave me a cursory glance. Just as I felt relief, I heard officers had found the money behind the vending machine over their radio. My stomach dropped. I realized I had been caught.

I sat at the restaurant table, my eyes darting around the room, trying to seem like a regular patron. My mind was racing; the adrenaline from the earlier robbery was now replaced with fear and a sense of impending doom. I ordered a steak, baked potato, salad, and a beer, trying to distract myself from the situation. But the food sat before me, barely touched; my appetite was gone. I couldn't help noticing the other patrons seemed carefree and unaware of the danger looming over my head.

Then, out of nowhere, a large officer walked up behind me and placed his giant hand on my shoulder. The weight of his hand felt like a ton of bricks. I knew then I was about to lose my freedom.

"You need to come with me for questioning," he said.

Walking down the hall, I felt everyone was watching me. Every step felt heavy and clumsy. Could they tell I had just robbed a bank? A detective and two FBI agents were waiting for me in one of the hotel's small conference rooms. Strangely, a sense of calm washed over me, even as the situation's gravity sank in. Oddly, I didn't ask what I was being detained for.

They sat me down in the room and left me there for what seemed like hours, though it was probably only minutes. I could hear the bustle of activity outside the door as officers searched my hotel room and rental car for evidence. They even brought in several bank tellers and other staff members to identify me.

Eventually, an FBI agent came in and read me my rights. Agent Moses said they were convinced they could make a compelling case against me and that, after reviewing the footage, they knew this wasn't my first bank robbery. My heart sank even farther. I felt betrayed by my arrogance in thinking I could get away with it.

Now, I was facing the possibility of spending significant time in prison. As I tried to keep my thoughts from spiraling out of control, one of the FBI agents leaned in and advised me to cooperate with the investigators and prosecutor for leniency.

I knew enough not to say anything that would incriminate me, so I nodded in agreement. The agents then led me out of the hotel, through the lobby, and past the swarm of reporters gathered in the parking lot. My heart pounded as I stepped into the back of the FBI vehicle, knowing my life was about to take a dramatic turn.

The drive to the Federal Bureau of Prison's Metropolitan Correctional Center was a blur. As we pulled up to the facility, I couldn't help but feel I was living a nightmare. I was fingerprinted, stripped of all my possessions, and booked into the prison as an inmate awaiting trial. The sounds of metal doors clanging shut and the sight of other inmates pacing in their cells made my heart sink even lower.

Sitting in my cell, I thought about what my life had become. The reality of my situation was hitting me hard.

The following day, my wife found out what had happened when local FBI agents in Tucson knocked on her door to search our house for evidence. Imagining what she was going through, knowing her husband had been arrested for bank robbery, made me feel even worse.

My first night in prison was nothing like I had ever experienced before. As the cell door clanged shut behind me, I was struck by the overpowering stench of sweat and desperation. But the most imposing presence in the room was the massive black man on the top bunk, his muscles bulging even in repose. It scared me when he stirred slightly, and I tried to make myself as small and unobtrusive as possible. The fatigue from the long day of interrogation and booking soon overtook me, and I fell into an uneasy sleep.

The following day, I woke feeling disoriented and unsure of where I was. As I looked around at the rough, hostile faces of the other inmates, it slowly dawned on me that I was in a completely foreign world. Then I learned *America's Most Wanted* had aired footage of my arrest the previous night; I could hear the inmates whispering about me.

As I stepped into the bustling general population, the atmosphere ignited with raucous jeers and provocative catcalls. I instantly became the center of attention, labeled as the "fresh meat" or the "newcomer" by my fellow inmates, with ominous predictions about my fate in the prison pecking order. Despite my apprehension, my stature as a six-foot-two, 230-pound individual granted me a reprieve from being seen as an easy target, sparing me from the horrors of sexual assault that often plagued newcomers.

Contrary to the sensationalized portrayals on television, there were no shortages of willing participants when it came to sexual encounters.

In reality, the majority of sexual assaults were driven by a desire for dominance rather than desperation. As for myself, I adopted a strategy of keeping a low profile, attempting to steer clear of trouble at every turn. Yet, in that harrowing first week, danger seemed to lurk around every corner, unveiling a disturbing reality. I bore witness to an unsettling number of brawls and brutal stabbings, events that surpassed my wildest nightmares. I felt as though I had descended into a living nightmare, with no certainty of ever emerging from the abyss. My life had plummeted to its lowest point. The first few days in prison were a total blur. It was like stepping into a new world I never thought I'd find myself in. Everything was new, and everything was scary. The rules were different, and the people were different. I had to learn how to navigate the institutional rules and each correctional officer's particular idiosyncrasies. The unwritten rules among the inmates were just as challenging to figure out.

I was determined to keep my head low and not draw any unwanted attention to myself from either the guards or the inmates. But at the same time, I couldn't help trying to figure out all the politics and power dynamics within the prison system. I spent my days watching the other inmates, observing their behavior, and trying to understand it all.

As the days turned into weeks, something strange began to happen. I started to adapt to the environment and understand the game's rules. I learned how to avoid troublemakers and befriend those who could help me. I even started to make some connections.

During this time, I made a decision that would change my life forever. Surrounded by chaos, I reflected on my life and the decisions that had led me to this place. I vowed to change and become a better person. I knew I had to take responsibility for my actions and the harm I had caused others. It was a pivotal moment.

As the days went by, I noticed a common theme among many of the inmates. They all had a victim mindset or mentality. They believed their past experiences and circumstances were responsible for their current situation. Like me, many had experienced challenging childhoods, and some had known even worse experiences with the justice system. But they all believed their behavior was justified and not their fault.

People with a victim mindset tend to see themselves as the targets of unfair treatment so they feel sorry for themselves. They focus on their problems rather than potential solutions, thinking themselves powerless, and they hold others responsible for their negative experiences.

During those long days of confinement, I began to reflect on my life and choices. I realized that I, too, had been living with a victim mindset. I saw myself as powerless and at the mercy of my external circumstances. I tended to blame others for my problems and avoided taking responsibility for my actions.

The statistics were daunting—an 85 percent recidivism rate for inmates after release. I knew I didn't want to be another statistic. I was determined to be among the 15 percent who never returned.

I knew I couldn't continue to live my life that way. If I wanted to break the cycle of incarceration and lead a successful life, I needed to take responsibility for my actions, thoughts, emotions, behaviors, and experiences. I needed to change how I viewed the world and my place in it.

I knew no one had forced me to rob those banks. I decided I had to take responsibility for my actions. I didn't intend to beat the charges, but I felt compelled to, for the first time, personally assess my mindset and beliefs.

It was a challenging process. I had to confront some hard truths about myself and my past. But I knew it was the only way to move forward and create something positive from this experience. I started reading books about personal growth and development and meditated regularly.

Despite the challenging environment, I saw the prison as an opportunity to grow and change. I didn't want to be another victim in a system designed to make people feel helpless and powerless. I wanted to take control of my life and future, and I was determined to do whatever it took to make that happen.

Looking back, I'm grateful for that moment of clarity in prison. It was the beginning of a journey leading me from prison to prosperity.

## Facing the Consequences of Decisions Made in a Victim Mindset

Reflecting on my experience, I realize how crucial it is to own our decisions and mindset. It's not always easy to admit we have made mistakes or our way of thinking may be holding us back, but it is necessary to improve our lives.

When we make decisions in a victim or disempowering mindset, we set ourselves up for consequences that can last for years or even a lifetime. It can be challenging to break free from this way of thinking, but it's never too late to start taking ownership of our lives.

The first step is to accept 100 percent responsibility for our actions and mindset. Blaming others or our circumstances for our problems is tempting, but this approach will only hold us back. When we take ownership of our lives, we gain control over our future.

The next step is to start changing the way we think and what we focus on. Our mindset plays a huge role in our lives, and a negative or disempowering attitude can limit our potential. We need to start focusing on positive and empowering thoughts and beliefs. This will help us make better decisions and take actions that move us toward our goals.

Establishing our standards, values, and principles is crucial to lasting change. When we know what we stand for and what is important to us, we can make decisions that align with those values. This helps us stay true to ourselves and avoid the mistakes that can come from living according to other people's expectations or societal pressure.

It's important to remember that change takes time. The consequences of our past decisions may be undone over time, and there is always time to start taking ownership and making positive changes. The journey may be difficult, but the rewards are worth it.

As retired astronaut, speaker, and philanthropist Ron Garan said, "We are limited only by our imagination and our will to act." We open ourselves to unlimited potential and possibility when we own our lives. It's up to us to decide what kind of life we want to create, and the first step is taking ownership of our decisions and mindset.

Recognize that turning your life around will take time. Time, patience, and perseverance are required to create meaningful change. You must be willing to work and make sacrifices to achieve your goals. But the good news is there is always time to start. No matter how old you are or how deep you are in your current circumstances, you have the power to change.

One of the most crucial steps is to accept 100 percent responsibility for your actions and the mindset that led to them. This means acknowledging you are in control of your life and solely responsible for the decisions you make. It's easy to blame our problems on external factors, but the truth is we have the power to change our lives. When we accept this responsibility, we become empowered to act and make a difference in our lives.

Another important aspect of taking ownership of your decisions is changing your thoughts. Your thoughts create your reality, so focusing on positive, empowering thoughts is essential. Instead of dwelling on past mistakes and failures, focus on what you can do now to improve your situation. You have the power to change your thoughts and choose to focus on the life you want to create.

Establishing standards, values, and principles is essential going forward. They serve as a roadmap to guide your actions and decisions. When you have a clear vision of what you want to achieve and what you stand for, it's easier to make choices that align with your goals.

Remember, there is always time to take ownership of your life and create meaningful change. Accepting responsibility for your actions and changing your mindset is vital to making lasting progress. With patience, perseverance, and a commitment to your goals, you can overcome the consequences of poor decisions and move toward a better future.

## The Danger of a Victim Mindset

When we approach life with a victim mindset, we surrender our power to outside circumstances and make decisions that are not in our best interest. We become reactive rather than proactive and blame others for our circumstances. The victim mindset is a way of thinking that emphasizes powerlessness, blame, and negativity. It is easy to fall into the trap of this mindset, particularly when we have faced hardship or adversity.

However, adopting a victim mindset can significantly undermine decision-making. It can lead to poor choices that perpetuate a cycle of negativity and disempowerment. For instance, we may engage in a self-destructive behavior like abusing alcohol and blame others for our drinking, using heredity, outside stress, or unfavorable circumstances to justify our actions rather than take responsibility and work to overcome our dependency.

Owning our thoughts and emotions is the key to breaking free from a victim mindset. We need to recognize we are responsible for our own lives and the decisions we make. We can choose our thoughts and actions and how we express our feelings, and it is up to us to make the most of that power.

It is also essential to recognize it may take time to turn our lives around, particularly if we have been living with a victim mindset for some time. But it's always worth the time to take ownership of our decisions and work toward a more positive future.

Many people have overcome serious challenges and achieved great success by avoiding the victim mindset. For instance, Oprah Winfrey grew up in poverty and faced numerous challenges, but she chose to take ownership of her life and use her experiences to help others.

By taking ownership of our decisions, we can break free from a victim mindset and move toward a more positive future.

### Taking Ownership of Your Decisions

Taking ownership of your decisions is crucial in creating positive life changes. It's natural to want to blame external circumstances or other people for the difficulties we face, but doing so keeps us stuck in a victim mindset that prevents us from taking action to improve our situation. In my personal experience, I had to accept that my past decisions and the victim mindset that led to them had landed me in prison. It was a harsh reality but also a wake-up call that forced me to take ownership of my past and start making positive changes for my future.

Recognizing the effects of past decisions on your current circumstances is the first step in taking ownership of your life. You must be honest with yourself about your decisions and how they've contributed to your current situation. It's easy to ignore or justify past mistakes, but doing so only perpetuates the cycle of negative consequences. Instead, you must face them head-on and recognize how they've led you to where you are today.

Once you've identified your past choices and their outcomes, it's essential to recognize the role of mindset in decision-making. Our mindset and beliefs shape our choices, so examining and reframing them is crucial to making more empowering decisions. By shifting your mindset and beliefs, you can make better choices that lead to positive outcomes.

Taking responsibility for past decisions and their consequences is a critical step. Doing so means accepting responsibility for the outcomes of your choices, even if doing so is difficult or painful.

Real-life examples of people who have taken ownership of their past and made positive changes are abundant. Look to successful people who have faced adversity, assumed responsibility for their past, and used it to fuel positive change. Brené Brown, a renowned researcher on vulnerability and shame, overcame her struggles with vulnerability to help others embrace their vulnerability as a path to personal growth. Frank William Abagnale, the con artist who was the subject of the 2002 movie *Catch Me If You Can*, went on to help others prevent fraud.

Taking ownership of your past choices and their consequences is not an easy process, but it is necessary for creating positive change. By recognizing the implications of past decisions, reframing your mindset, and taking responsibility for your choices, you can create a brighter future. Remember, it's never too late to change.

## Setting Personal Standards, Values, and Principles for Decision-Making

Reflecting on my journey in facing the consequences of my decisions, I realize the most crucial step was accepting 100 percent responsibility for my actions. It wasn't easy, but it was necessary. It took me some time to turn my life around, and I had to start by setting personal standards, values, and principles for decision-making.

When you take ownership of your choices, you see the power of a growth mindset and continuous learning. You realize every decision you make can either move you toward your goals or away from them. By developing a growth mindset, you can see failures as opportunities to learn and grow instead of setbacks that define you.

Creating a positive, empowering environment and support system is a key to turning your life around. When you surround yourself with people who uplift and support you, it becomes easier to make positive changes. You need people who will hold you accountable, encourage you, and help you stay on track.

Taking action is the most critical step of all. It's not enough to have good intentions or to plan for change. You have to take action toward positive change. You have to decide to take small steps every day toward your goals, even when it's hard.

It may take time, but it's worth it. Turning your life around and creating a better future is worth the effort. I've repeatedly seen that taking ownership of your decisions, setting personal standards and values, developing a growth mindset, creating a positive environment and support system, and taking action toward positive change are essential steps in creating the life you want.

So, I encourage you to take that first step toward positive change today, regardless of your current circumstances. It may be challenging, but it's worth it. And remember, there is always time to start. With the right mindset and support system, you can overcome the consequences of your past decisions and create a bright future.

## Self-Reflection

This chapter covers the importance of taking ownership of your decisions. You've learned the importance of accepting responsibility for past choices, changing your mindset, and setting personal standards and values for decision-making. But the real progress comes from putting these concepts into action. That's why I invite you to take the time to answer the following questions. By writing out your answers, you'll be able to provoke pattern changes in how you face the consequences of previous decisions and adversity in the future. You'll have access to new tools and ways of changing your mindset, ultimately empowering you to create a brighter future. So, take some time to reflect, and let's get started!

## Questions to Reflect On

- Which specific decisions that you made in the past led to your current circumstances?
- How can you reframe your mindset to empower yourself and take ownership of your decisions in the future?
- What are your personal standards, values, and principles for decision-making, and how have they served you in the past?
- In what ways have you fallen into a victim mindset in the past, and how have you perpetuated negative cycles as a result?
- How can you develop a growth mindset and see failures as opportunities to learn and grow rather than setbacks that define you?

- What steps can you take right now to create a positive environment and support system to help you take action toward positive change?

## Summary

- **Take ownership of your decisions:** Accept 100 percent responsibility for your actions and the mindset that led to them. Acknowledge that you control your life and are responsible for your choices.

- **Change your mindset:** Your thoughts create reality, so focus on positive, empowering thoughts. Focus on what you want to create instead of dwelling on past mistakes and failures.

- **Establish your standards, values, and principles:** These serve as a roadmap to guide your actions and decisions. When you have a clear vision of what you want to achieve and what you stand for, it's easier to make choices that align with your goals.

- **Beware of a victim mindset:** A victim mindset emphasizes powerlessness, blame, and negativity, which can significantly undermine decision-making. Instead, own your thoughts and emotions, and recognize that you are responsible for your life and your decisions.

- **Recognize the effects of past decisions:** Be honest with yourself about your decisions and how they've contributed to your current situation. Face your mistakes and recognize how they've led you to where you are today.

- **Take action:** Having good intentions or planning for change is not enough. You have to take action toward positive change. Take small daily steps toward your goals, even when it's hard, and surround yourself with people who uplift and support you.

## Conclusion

Remember, there is always time to change and turn your life around. Taking ownership of your decisions and developing a growth mindset can propel you toward your goals and help you overcome adversity. Recognizing the consequences of your past decisions, setting personal standards and values, reframing your mindset, and taking action toward positive change are essential steps in creating the life you want. Embrace your mistakes, learn from them, and use them to fuel your growth. You can create a brighter future by taking ownership of your life. So, go out there and start making the change you want to see in your life. Remember, you have what it takes to succeed, and the world is waiting for you to unleash your potential.

# UNLEASHING YOUR OWN POTENTIAL

with Robert Henry

# 6

# SETTING A PERSONAL STANDARD: HOW TO UNLEASH YOUR POTENTIAL

*"In the midst of winter, I found there was within me an invincible summer."*

— Albert Camus

After a year-long negotiation with the federal prosecutor following my arrest, we reached a pivotal plea agreement. This unique deal demanded full disclosure of every detail regarding my criminal activities, which, in a daring spree, spanned ten bank heists across the sun-soaked landscapes of Southern Arizona and Southern California. My exploits had me crossing the jurisdictional lines of four distinct federal territories. As difficult as it was to come clean about my crimes, I knew it was the right thing to do. It was the only way to begin making amends and rebuilding my life.

To my surprise, one of the positive outcomes of this situation was that the probation officer who had caused me so much grief was finally investigated. It turns out I wasn't the only one who had suffered at his hands. His corrupt ways had caught up with him, and he faced several charges—including the appalling accusation of pimping out his female probationers. I was horrified to hear he expected these vulnerable women to continue being prostitutes and pay him a cut of their earnings.

Unease filled me as the plea agreement was read. The prosecutor stipulated I would only be charged with one count for each jurisdiction instead of ten individual counts. At first, I was relieved—it felt like a weight had been lifted off my shoulders. But that relief was short-lived when the prosecutor recommended the court sentence me to seventy-eight months for each of the four counts.

My fate was in the judge's hands. It would be up to him to determine whether I served my sentences concurrently or consecutively. The difference was stark—if my sentences were to run concurrently, it would mean serving six-and-a-half years total, or five years with "good behavior." If the judge decided my sentences would run consecutively, it would mean serving twenty-six years, or twenty-two years and three months with good behavior. If that was the case, I would be released when I was forty-seven.

The weight of the situation was palpable—the decision was in the judge's hands, and my future hung in the balance. The thought of spending more than two decades behind bars was overwhelming.

As I sat in the courtroom, waiting for the judge's decision, my heart felt like it was about to burst through my chest. I could hear the murmur of other inmates as they received their sentences—one to three years seemed to be the norm. I couldn't help but feel anxious as I waited for my turn to stand before the judge.

When it was my turn, the judge looked sternly at me, eyes bearing on me with intense scrutiny. My heart raced as I listened intently for the phrases that would determine my fate: concurrently or consecutively. The words hung heavily in my mind as I held my breath.

And then he spoke.

"Concurrently."

The relief that washed over me was overwhelming. I was so grateful I almost didn't hear the rest of the sentence. A remarkable twist unfolded—the judge granted me a "downward departure" from the hefty seventy-eight-month sentence initially on the table. Let me break it down: In the world of federal sentencing, a "downward departure" is when a judge decides to go easier on a defendant than what the rulebook suggests. It's a bit like a "Get Out of Jail Free Card" from the *Monopoly* game but in real life.

This isn't your everyday decision, mind you. Judges have the power to choose this path when they believe it's warranted, based on the unique details of the case. In my situation, it was like a ray of unexpected mercy shining through. Maybe the judge saw the turbulence I'd faced, including a run-in with a crooked probation officer. I'll never know for sure, but I was deeply thankful for the compassion shown. As the reality of my situation set in, I realized I would be released before I turned thirty. The thought of still having a life after prison filled me with hope, and I knew it was a second chance I couldn't afford to squander.

Looking back, I'm sure my reaction to the judge's sentence must have appeared strange to onlookers. But, at that moment, I was overcome with gratitude, and I profusely thanked the judge for his decision. It was a moment I would never forget and marked the possibility of a new beginning in my life.

The time in prison that followed was a turning point for me. It was a time of reflection and self-discovery that allowed me to see the world in a new light. One of my most significant realizations, as already mentioned, was the prevalence of victim mindsets in the prison population. I had also fallen into that mindset, though I didn't realize it at the time.

I had come to believe my problems were caused by external factors—other people, circumstances, or events—and I had little control over them. My victim mindset led me to feel angry, frustrated, and hopeless, and that made it difficult for me to take action to improve my situation.

But the truth is I was not alone. People with victim mindsets are all around us—they may be our friends, family, or even ourselves. The consequences of that mindset are profound, leading us to feel a sense of entitlement or helplessness and to blame others for our problems.

The most challenging thing about having a victim mindset is we may not even know we have it. We may have developed it to cope with difficult life circumstances. We may see our negative patterns of thinking and behavior as a result of external factors rather than a choice or a habit we have developed.

Breaking free from this mindset can be difficult, but taking ownership of our lives and creating a better future for ourselves is essential. The first step is to recognize and acknowledge we have a victim mindset and understand this thinking pattern is not serving us.

Confronting our thinking patterns and behavior can be uncomfortable, but that confrontation is necessary to grow and improve. We must be willing to challenge our beliefs and take responsibility for our actions, even if it means stepping out of our comfort zone.

In those initial days after my arrest, I had an eye-opening moment. I suddenly saw I'd been trapped in a victim mindset. This realization changed everything, including my response when an opportunity to escape presented itself.

Choosing to stay put was no walk in the park, let me tell you. But it was also my first step toward taking control of my life and embarking on a journey of self-improvement. That decision was a turning point, the very beginning of a whole new chapter in my life. Realizing all my decisions and actions had been made from a victim mindset was a tough pill to swallow. It felt like I had abdicated control over my life and future to others, which was gut-wrenching. But, at that moment, I decided to take 100 percent responsibility for my life—including my choices.

Taking 100 percent responsibility meant taking control of my thoughts and emotions and choosing to respond to challenges and adversity proactively and positively. It meant facing the abuse I had experienced in my childhood—both physical and sexual—and accepting the pain and trauma that came with it. It meant acknowledging my abandonment after losing my father at a young age and coming to terms with the heartbreak of being cheated on by my ex-wife.

It meant owning up to my mistakes—the decisions that led to my arrest at the advertising company, the experience with the corrupt probation officer, and the bank robberies that ultimately landed me in prison. It was difficult, but it was essential if I wanted to move forward and take control of my life.

Taking 100 percent responsibility was not just about accepting what had happened to me—it was about acknowledging that I had a choice in how I responded. It meant being proactive in my approach to life rather than reactive. It meant taking control of my destiny and working toward a better future.

The path wasn't easy, and many moments I struggled to maintain my focus and stay true to my commitments. But I knew that taking responsibility for my life was essential to creating a better future. That decision allowed me to move beyond the victim mindset that had held me back for so long and to take control of my destiny.

Some people may take issue with my statement that I had to take responsibility for the abuse I experienced in my childhood—both physical and sexual. But here's the thing: Taking responsibility doesn't mean accepting blame for what happened. Instead, it means recognizing that while I may not have had control over the events, I do have control over how I respond to them.

Taking 100 percent responsibility for your life and experiences means accepting you are in control of your thoughts, feelings, and actions—and taking ownership of the outcomes that result from them. It means recognizing you can create the life you want and you are responsible for your choices, regardless of your circumstances or past experiences.

Personally, taking responsibility was a critical turning point in my life. I realized if I wanted to take control of my future and the direction of my life, I had to change how I thought. That's why the first thing I did was decide to create a new standard for myself.

I consciously chose to no longer respond to external circumstances based on emotion or rely on the old thinking patterns my upbringing had influenced. I had to look hard at the thoughts and beliefs holding me back for so long and actively work to change them.

I remember the moment when everything changed for me. I made a simple yet profound decision: I would be a good man. Period, No matter what.

It was a radical shift in my mindset that meant I would no longer justify my actions based on being a victim but instead take responsibility for my choices and strive to be the best version of myself I could be. It meant working hard to learn as much as possible and becoming a lifelong student of personal development and growth.

But it wasn't just about learning. It was about putting that knowledge into action daily and making a conscious choice to be the kind of man I wanted to be. It was about looking at every situation and every choice through a different lens and asking, "What would a good and honorable man do in this situation?"

Transforming my life went far beyond reading books or changing my mindset. It was about committing to living with honor and integrity, doing the right thing even when it was hard, and never giving up on my dreams.

I knew changing my mindset would take work. It would require being honest with myself in ways I had never been before. It meant letting go of old patterns that no longer served me and challenging myself to grow in new and uncomfortable ways.

But I was determined to do it. I knew if I wanted to make the most of my life, I had to make this shift in my mindset. I had to look for the gift and the opportunity in every situation.

Being in prison was one of the most challenging times of my life, but it also offered me a rare opportunity: the chance to strip away the outside world's distractions and focus on personal growth. I read 700 books while in prison, diving deep into personal development, psychology, and philosophy.

It wasn't easy, but it was worth it. The decision to be a good man, take responsibility for my life, and actively work toward my personal growth has paid off in ways I never imagined. I found a newfound sense of purpose and passion that propelled me forward. As I reflect on my journey, I am grateful for the life I created. It is a life filled with meaning, direction, and joy. I wake up daily with a sense of purpose, knowing I am doing what is right and helping others build the lives they've dreamed of.

Early on, I read many self-help books exploring the concept of mindset and how it affects our approach to success and personal growth.

There are many books that introduce the concept of mindset and explore the difference between fixed and growth mindsets. With a fixed mindset, a person believes their abilities and intelligence are fixed and they have little control over their potential for growth and success. In contrast, with a growth mindset, people believe their abilities and intelligence can be developed through hard work, practice, and perseverance.

A fixed mindset can be detrimental to personal growth and success while a growth mindset can lead to greater resilience, creativity, and achievement. Many examples exist of how individuals with different perspectives approach challenges, setbacks, and criticism.

One book that greatly influenced my growth in prison and upon release was *Awaken the Giant Within* by Tony Robbins. This self-help book emphasizes the importance of taking control of your life and creating the results you want through developing empowering beliefs, habits, and strategies. A key concept in the book is creating a personal standard for yourself.

According to Robbins, creating a personal standard involves defining your values and the principles that guide your decisions and behavior. He encourages readers to identify areas where they want improvement and commit to a higher standard of conduct. This process could involve setting specific goals, establishing empowering rituals and habits, and adopting a mindset of excellence and commitment to growth.

Robbins also emphasizes the importance of taking consistent action toward your goals, even when it's difficult or un comfortable. He encourages readers to cultivate the mindset of a "peak performer" and focus on developing the mental and emotional toughness needed to overcome obstacles and achieve success.

As I reflect on my journey, I realize that by consistently adhering to the standard I set for myself, I was able to develop emotional maturity and resilience, which I had never experienced before. It was challenging, especially in prison, where that standard was constantly tested. But the long-term payoff of holding on to my standard was priceless.

One instance that stands out in my mind was when an officer was escorting me down a hallway, and we came across an open office door, revealing a possible escape route. I was in a cold sweat, my mind racing with the temptation to run. But I knew succumbing to that temptation would betray my commitment to my standard. So, despite the fear and uncertainty of my situation, I stood my ground and did not take the escape opportunity.

The officer noticed I was visibly shaken and escorted me back to my high-security floor. Later, I learned the same officer was promoted to the position of determining which institution inmates would be transferred to next. He had the power to send me to a medium-high security facility where violence, drugs, and gangs were rampant. However, he recognized my commitment to upholding my standard and sent me to a lower-security institution.

This experience taught me that even in the most challenging and unpredictable situations, adhering to my standards and values was the key to maintaining my integrity and staying on the path of personal growth. It's not just about avoiding the negative consequences of our actions but also about reaping the long-term benefits of living a life that aligns with our values and beliefs.

Fortunately, the officer sent me to a medium-low security prison with mostly non-violent inmates serving less than five years. Was this a result of my decision to do the right thing, take responsibility, and not escape? I'll never know, but I can tell you that one of the most valuable decisions I've made is to set a standard for myself to live by.

Christians know this as "What would Jesus do?" Similarly, whenever I questioned what I should do, I asked myself, "What would a good and honorable man do in this situation?"

The new standard I created for myself stated:

- I would be a good man.
- I would be an honorable man.
- I would be brutally honest with myself and no longer tolerate a victim or "fixed mindset."
- I would become a lifelong student, continually learning to be my best.
- I would look to see the gift or opportunity in every situation rather than look for the negative.

Adhering to my new standard sometimes brought me short-term discomfort or pain, but it always proved to be the best decision in the long run. Becoming a lifelong student, continually learning to be the best I could be, and looking for the gift or opportunity in every situation rather than focusing on the negative was a profound shift in my mindset, and it changed my life.

## Personal Standards Are the Foundation of Personal Growth and Unleashing Your Potential

Setting a personal standard is the foundation of personal growth and unleashing your potential. Personal standards define how we act and determine how we navigate life's challenges. They set the tone for our behaviors and guide us through life's ups and downs.

Think of personal standards as the compass that guides your journey. When you set a personal standard, you create a roadmap for your life. It gives you a clear direction of where you're headed and helps you focus your energy on what matters most. By establishing a set of values, principles, and standards, you declare who you are and what you stand for.

The power of setting a personal standard comes from the clarity, direction, and purpose it provides. When you have a personal standard, you know exactly what you want and where you're headed. You can say no to distractions that don't align with your values and goals. You can focus your energy on what matters and make decisions confidently.

But you need to do more than set a personal standard. You must also commit to living up to your standards every day. You must hold yourself accountable to the highest level of integrity and never settle for less than you deserve. You must constantly strive to be the best version of yourself and never stop growing and learning.

It's important to understand that setting a personal standard is not a one-time event. It's a process that requires ongoing attention and effort. You must be willing to examine your life regularly, assess your progress, and make adjustments as needed. This process can be challenging. It requires brutal honesty and facing the truth about who you are and who you want to become. It can sometimes be uncomfortable and even painful, but the reward is worth the effort. When you set a personal standard and commit to it, you unleash your potential and create a life of purpose, fulfillment, and joy.

Personal standards are the foundation of personal growth and unleashing your potential. By setting a personal standard, you create a roadmap for your life, focus your energy, and take control of your destiny. The power of setting a personal standard comes from the clarity, direction, and purpose it provides. Remember, the choice is always yours.

## Understanding Personal Standards

Setting a personal standard for myself was the most critical turning point in my journey from prison to prosperity. I had hit rock bottom and had no idea where to turn until I realized my mindset and behavior were the root cause of my situation. I had to take 100 percent responsibility for my life, thoughts, and actions. And that's when I decided to set a personal standard for myself.

Personal standards are the foundation of personal growth and unleashing your potential. Your values, principles, and behaviors guide your decisions and actions. Personal standards are the rules and expectations you set based on your beliefs, experiences, and goals. It's easy to get sidetracked by others' opinions or to compare yourself to others, but when you have personal standards, they keep you on track and in alignment with your true self.

People who set high personal standards create a roadmap for their lives. They focus their energy and take control of their destinies. They clearly understand what they want to achieve and the paths they need to take to get there. When you set personal standards, you give yourself direction and a sense of purpose. Your standards help you stay focused and motivated, even when the road ahead is challenging.

The power of setting a personal standard comes from the clarity, direction, and purpose it provides. When you know your personal standards, you clearly know what you stand for and what you will not tolerate. You have a framework for making decisions and a set of expectations to which you hold yourself accountable. This framework provides a solid foundation for building a meaningful, fulfilling life aligned with your values.

Personal standards can help you cultivate a growth mindset, overcome limiting beliefs, and live a life of purpose and fulfillment. When you set high personal standards, you challenge yourself to be your best self. You push yourself to grow, learn, and become the person you were meant to be. When you live up to your personal standards, you experience an unparalleled sense of pride, accomplishment, and fulfillment.

Remember, personal standards are the foundation of personal growth and can be the key to unlocking your true potential.

To truly unleash your potential, you must have a growth mindset. That means believing your abilities and intelligence can be developed and improved over time. With a growth mindset, you can embrace challenges and setbacks as opportunities for growth and learning. Personal standards are a key component of a growth mindset because they help you stay focused on what is important and avoid getting distracted by external factors.

In my own life, setting personal standards was critical to turning my life around. By accepting 100 percent responsibility for my actions and the mindset that led to my decisions, I could take control of my life and establish new standards, values, and principles to live by. It wasn't easy and took time, but by focusing on my personal standards, I could cultivate a growth mindset and unleash my potential.

Personal standards are critical to unleashing your potential. They are the foundation of personal growth and can help you achieve your goals and unleash your potential.

## The Benefits of Setting a Personal Standard

Setting a personal standard gave me clarity and direction. In addition to providing direction, setting a personal standard fostered self-discipline, self-accountability, and self-motivation. It enabled me to take full responsibility for my life and empowered me to unleash my potential and navigate the ups and downs of life with confidence and clarity.

## How to Set a Personal Standard

I began by identifying my core values and beliefs. I took the time to think about what mattered most to me and what principles I wanted to live by. It was a challenging exercise but crucial to understanding who I was and who I wanted to become.

After defining my core values and beliefs, I defined what success meant. I set specific goals that aligned with my values and committed to a higher standard of conduct. I understood it was not enough to set goals; I had to commit to achieving them by holding myself to my standard.

I've developed some empowering rituals and habits that help me stay on track with my goals and maintain a high personal standard. Here are a few examples of the daily habits I follow:

1. **Morning Gratitude:** Each day begins with a moment of reflection. I focus on the aspects of my life that I'm truly grateful for. This simple practice sets a positive tone for the day ahead.
2. **Expressing Gratitude:** Throughout the day, I actively seek opportunities to express sincere gratitude in various ways. It's a small act that has a big impact on my mindset and interactions.
3. **Managing Negative Emotions:** I take responsibility for managing negative emotions like frustration and anger. When these feelings arise, I pause to ask myself why I felt that way. Often, it's because of unspoken or unrealistic expectations. Shifting my focus to gratitude or appreciation helps diffuse negativity.

Now, let me illustrate the power of being proactive with an example. During a recent conference with my team, we had a tight lunch break schedule. Instead of leaving it to chance, I called local restaurants in advance to ensure they could accommodate us within our time constraints. This simple act spared my team from stress, frustration, and late returns to the conference, while others faced those challenges.

When you proactively manage your life and emotions, and communicate your expectations clearly, it's astonishing how much smoother and more harmonious your experiences become.

In every aspect of my life, I strive to ensure that my actions align with my values and beliefs. It's essential to me that every decision I make and action I take reflects my personal standard. This process made me realize my personal standard was more than just setting and achieving goals. It was about making a conscious effort to be the best version of myself and to live a fulfilling, purposeful life. It was about taking responsibility for my life and holding myself accountable for my actions.

## Overcoming Challenges and Obstacles

Setting a personal standard is a challenging task. It requires a lot of discipline, consistency, and resilience. Inevitably, setbacks, failures, and temptations will challenge your commitment. But remember, you have already come a long way and should not give up now.

When you face challenges, take a deep breath and remember your *why* and purpose. Why are you doing this? Why is this important to you? Reconnect with your core values and beliefs, and stay true to your personal standard. It will guide you in times of doubt, fear, or uncertainty.

Moreover, seeking support and accountability from others who share your values and goals can be invaluable. These people can provide feedback, share their experiences and wisdom, and help you stay motivated. People who have walked a similar path can be your mentors, coaches, or peers. They can offer a different perspective, challenge your assumptions, and help you see things in a new light.

But ultimately, it's up to you to overcome challenges and obstacles and stay true to your personal standard. As you face these challenges, you will grow stronger, wiser, and more resilient. You will learn from your mistakes, refine your approach, and find new ways to unleash your potential.

Setting a personal standard is a lifelong journey, not a destination. You will keep refining, adjusting, and expanding it as you grow and evolve. But as long as you stay committed to your personal standard, you will stay on the path of personal growth and unleash your potential.

Feel free to ask for help or to seek guidance from experts in your field. Look to others who have already accomplished your goals, and learn from them. It can be incredibly motivating to know someone has already achieved what you are working toward and it is possible for you too.

Finally, be prepared to adjust your personal standard as you grow and evolve. As you achieve your goals and reach new heights, your standard will naturally rise to meet your new level of success. Remember to continue learning, growing, challenging yourself, and striving for excellence in everything you do.

## Embracing Growth and Learning

Setting a personal standard is not just about setting up some principles and values to live by; it's a continuous growth, improvement, and learning process. It's essential to recognize your personal standard is not set in stone, and as you grow and evolve, so will your standard. The key is to embrace the journey, be open to new experiences, and continually learn and improve.

A growth mindset means you embrace growth. You are willing to learn how to develop your abilities and talents through hard work, dedication, and persistence. It's understanding your intelligence and talent are not fixed but can be developed through learning and practice. This mindset helps you overcome obstacles and setbacks and fuels motivation and perseverance.

To embrace growth and learning, you must be open to new experiences, seek new challenges, and step out of your comfort zone. You must also reflect on your progress, celebrate your successes, and learn from your failures. Taking time to assess your progress regularly allows you to recognize what's working and what's not, enabling you to adjust your personal standard and stay on track.

Remember that setting a personal standard is not a one-time event. It's an ongoing process that requires consistent effort, discipline, and resilience. You must stay committed to your values, beliefs, and goals, seek support and accountability from others, and be willing to make adjustments and adapt as you grow and evolve. Doing so unleashes your potential and helps you achieve your goals and live a life of purpose and fulfillment.

## Self-Reflection

This chapter has explored the power of setting a personal standard and how it can help you unleash your potential. You have learned that personal standards are the foundation of personal growth and guide your decisions and actions. It is time to act to apply what you have learned. Real progress comes when you take the time to reflect and answer the questions below, which are designed to provoke pattern and thinking changes. This process will provide you with new tools and ways of developing and using your personal standards when facing adversity. I invite you to reflect and answer the questions below—this exercise will help you grow and unleash your potential.

**Questions to Reflect On**

- What are your core values and beliefs, and how can you use them to set a personal standard that guides your decisions and actions?
- How have your past decisions and mindset influenced the adversity you have faced, and what can you do to take 100 percent responsibility for your actions moving forward?
- What is your definition of success, and what kind of person do you want to be? How can you use your personal standard to align your actions with your goals and live a life of purpose and fulfillment?
- What habits and rituals do you have in place that support your personal standard, and how can you create new ones to empower your growth and development?
- When faced with challenges and setbacks, how can you reconnect with your core values and beliefs, stay true to your personal standard, and seek support and accountability from others who share your values and goals?
- How can you use your personal standard as a dynamic

framework for growth and development, reflecting on your progress, celebrating your successes, and learning from your failures to continually adjust your personal standard to reflect your evolving values, beliefs, and goals?

## Summary

- Identify the core values and beliefs that guide your decisions and actions.
- Define what success means to you and what kind of person you want to be.
- Establish empowering rituals and habits that support your personal standard and align with your goals.
- Use your personal standard to make decisions and guide your actions.
- Seek support and accountability from others who share your values and goals.
- Embrace a growth mindset, be open to new experiences, and continually learn and improve, adjusting your personal standard to reflect your evolving values, beliefs, and goals.

## Conclusion

As we wrap up this session on setting a personal standard and unleashing your potential, I want to remind you that your past does not define you—your potential remains limitless. No matter what challenges you faced or will face in the future, you can overcome them and achieve greatness. By setting a personal standard, clarifying your vision and purpose, and aligning your actions with your values and goals, you can create a roadmap for your life and take control of your destiny. Remember to embrace growth and learning, seek support from others who share your values and goals, and take consistent action toward your dreams. Your personal standard is the foundation of your personal growth, and unleashing your potential is a lifelong journey. So, embrace the journey, stay true to yourself, and strive for your desired life. The power to unleash your potential is within you. Go out there and make it happen.

# UNLEASHING YOUR OWN POTENTIAL

with Robert Henry

# 7

# CHOOSING TO THRIVE: THE POWER OF DAILY RITUALS AND FOCUSING ON THE PRESENT

*"The secret of your success is found in your daily routine."*

— John C. Maxwell

Shortly after my sentencing, I was transferred to the Federal Correctional Institution, Safford (FCI Safford), a low-security United States federal prison for male inmates in Arizona. The Federal Bureau of Prisons, a United States Department of Justice division, operates it. FCI Safford is located in southeastern Arizona, seven miles south of the city of Safford, 127 miles northeast of Tucson, and 165 miles east of Phoenix.

As I sat in the holding cell with eight other inmates, I couldn't help being afraid. I had been sentenced to five years in prison, and I knew life in prison would be tough. The thought of spending years away from my family and friends was daunting, and the prospect of facing dangerous criminals was terrifying. But then, an older, grizzled inmate named Mike sat beside me. What he said changed my life forever.

Mike had spent almost thirty years in and out of prison, and he had learned a thing or two about survival. He looked at me, sizing me up, and asked if this was my first time in Federal prison. When I told him it was, he gave me a knowing nod and said, "Listen, kid, you're scared, and that's okay. But you have to learn to trust your gut instincts. Over time, you'll find they're usually right."

As I looked out into the prison yard, I saw inmates bench-pressing 405 pounds like it was nothing and felt even more intimidated. But Mike reassured me I would be okay. He told me to choose my friends wisely, and I would likely make lifelong bonds with one or two inmates. He said I needed to divorce myself from the outside world as soon as possible and focus on what I could control.

And then he said something that surprised me. He said I should make several shivs to hide throughout the prison for protection.

"Shiv" is slang for any sharp, pointed object used as a knife. A shiv can be created from anything, ranging from a shard of glass to a hardened, sharpened toothbrush handle. Similarly, "shank" refers to a makeshift knife-like weapon, and the two terms are often used interchangeably. I was hesitant at first, but he assured me it was unlikely I would ever have to use one. But simply knowing I could protect myself would give me confidence.

I remembered what Mike said and focused on what I could control. I quickly created a daily routine to help me get through the next four years. I woke at 5:30 a.m., meditated, and went to the gym before work. All inmates were required to work in some capacity, and I was fortunate to land a job at the prison factory (UNICOR). But I didn't stop there. I read more than seven hundred books, completed my GED, and took trade classes, including carpentry, and college courses about business and construction management.

Mike was right about one thing: I did make several friends I still keep in touch with. The daily routine I established helped the time go by much quicker, and I felt like I was accomplishing something each day. I gained a new appreciation for life and promised myself I would make the most of it once I was released. When the day finally came and I was released from prison, I felt like a new person. I was grateful for the second chance I had been given, and I knew I had the tools to make something of myself. I learned when life hands you a tough situation, you can crumble or rise to the occasion. I had chosen to rise to the occasion—which made all the difference.

Today, years later, I look back on my time in prison with gratitude. It was a difficult time, but it taught me some valuable lessons I still carry. It taught me the power of daily rituals, focusing on the present, and making the most of what I had. It taught me there is always hope, even in the darkest moments. And it taught me anything is possible with determination and the right mindset.

I hope this chapter will inspire others going through tough times. Whether you're facing a difficult time in your personal life or struggling to achieve your goals, remember you have the power to choose how you respond. You can choose to give up or rise to the occasion. You can focus on what you can control or dwell on what you can't. And you can choose to create a daily routine that helps you make the most of each day.

Making the right choices is not always easy, but it's always worth it. Looking back on my life, I'm grateful for the tough times because they helped me become the person I am today. And I'm grateful for people like Mike who came into my life and helped me see the way forward. So, if you're facing tough times, take heart. You always have hope. Just remember to trust your gut instincts, choose your friends wisely, and focus on what you can control. And, most importantly, never give up.

**Choosing to Thrive**

Through daily rituals, we can create structure and purpose and take control of our time and energy. Daily rituals can help us cultivate positive habits, increase focus and productivity, and improve our well-being. As a result, we can unlock our full potential and achieve our goals.

"Focusing on the present" is another key life lesson. In a world filled with distractions and stress, losing sight of what's truly important is easy. But by staying present and focused, we can make the most of each moment and avoid feeling overwhelmed by life's challenges. The authors I mentioned above all agree about the importance of focusing on the present. Brené Brown, for example, encourages readers to practice mindfulness and gratitude to stay present and connected to their lives. Simon Sinek emphasizes the power of purpose and vision to stay focused and motivated.

By focusing on the present, we can learn to appreciate the beauty of life, savor the small moments, and avoid getting bogged down by worries about the past or future. Focusing on the present can help us stay calm and centered in difficult moments and make better decisions that are aligned with our values and goals.

## Trusting Your Instincts to Make the Right Choices

We face countless big and small choices that can ultimately shape our future. Sometimes, we feel lost, unsure of which path to take, and unable to decide. This is where the power of developing our instincts comes in because doing so can help us make the right choices and lead us toward a thriving life.

As I learned in prison, trusting our instincts is essential to choosing to thrive. Our instincts are our body's unconscious signals; we must learn to recognize them and decipher their meaning. They provide an immediate and natural response often based on experience, knowledge, and values. The better we listen to our instincts, the more accurate and reliable they become.

In the face of difficult choices, our instincts can decide. They allow us to make quick decisions in high-pressure situations without overthinking—overthinking can often lead to indecisiveness or paralysis by analysis. However, that does not mean we should act recklessly or impulsively. Instead, it is essential to acknowledge and respect our instincts and use them to inform our decisions in a balanced way.

By relying on our instincts, we can reap the benefits of confidently making informed choices. Instinct can also help us avoid situations that may not be the best for us, protecting us from harm or negative outcomes. Trusting our instincts enables us to make choices that align with our values and goals, ultimately leading to a fulfilling life.

Trusting our instincts and relying on them to guide our choices may not always be easy. It requires patience, practice, and the willingness to listen to our inner voice. However, the more we develop our instincts and trust them, the more we can use them as a tool to thrive.

Overall, developing our instincts and trusting them is an important aspect of making the right choices. We can cultivate a more thriving and fulfilling life by acknowledging the importance of our instincts and relying on them in decision-making.

Here are some tips to get started:

- **Listen to your body:** Our instincts are often felt in our bodies, so pay attention to physical sensations such as tightness, butterflies, or calm. Take a moment to pause and notice what your body is telling you.

- **Reflect on experiences:** Our experiences shape our instincts, so remember when you trusted your instincts and made a good decision. What was it about the situation that felt right? How can you apply this to your current situation?

- **Practice decision-making:** The more decisions we make, the more we develop our instincts. Start with small choices and notice how your body responds. Over time, making decisions will become more natural and effortless.

- **Trust yourself:** It can be scary to trust your instincts, especially if they go against what others say or think. However, trust yourself and your judgment, and be confident your instincts will guide you to the right choice.

By developing and trusting our instincts, we can make the right choices, which will lead to a more fulfilling life. The process takes practice and patience, but the rewards are worth it. So, choose to thrive by focusing on your daily rituals and the present moment, and trust the power of your instincts to guide you to a life of purpose and meaning.

### Choose Wisely Whom You Associate With

Choosing whom we associate with is a crucial aspect of thriving. The people we surround ourselves with can greatly influence our lives either positively or negatively. As motivational speaker Jim Rohn once said, we become the average of the five people we spend the most time with. Here's why it's important to choose our friends wisely:

- **Our friends influence our thoughts and behaviors:** Friends can significantly influence our thoughts and behavior, often without realizing it. If we surround ourselves with negative, toxic people, we may start to adopt their negative mindsets and behaviors. On the other hand, if we surround ourselves with positive, uplifting people, we are more likely to adopt their positive outlook and behavior.

- **Our friends affect our energy:** Our friends can either lift us up or bring us down. Spending time with people who drain our energy can leave us exhausted and unmotivated. On the other hand, spending time with people who energize us and inspire us can leave us feeling invigorated and ready to take on the world.

- **Our friends can influence our success:** If we surround ourselves with successful and driven people, we are more likely to be successful. Conversely, if we surround ourselves with people who are negative and unmotivated, they may limit our ability to achieve our goals.

So, how can we choose friends who lift us up and help us thrive? Here are some strategies to consider:

- **Join groups or communities aligned with your interests and values:** This can be a great way to meet like-minded people who share your passion for a particular activity or cause.

- **Be intentional about whom you spend time with:** Pay attention to how you feel after spending time with certain people. It may be time to reevaluate the relationship if you feel drained or negative.

- **Seek positive, uplifting people:** Look for people who inspire, challenge, and support you. These are the people who will help you thrive.

- **Be a good friend yourself:** To attract positive, uplifting people, we must be positive and uplifting. Be a good friend and you will attract good friends in return.

We can thrive and achieve our goals by choosing our friends wisely and surrounding ourselves with positive, uplifting people. It takes effort and intention, but the rewards are immeasurable.

## Embracing Daily Rituals

Every day we can either drift through the day aimlessly or take control of our lives through the power of daily rituals. Rituals are the cornerstone of our lives, and they help us develop habits that create the foundation for our success.

Daily rituals are incredibly beneficial because they help us stay focused, eliminate distractions, and bring us closer to our goals. By incorporating daily rituals into our lives, we can create structure, reduce anxiety, and improve our overall well-being. When we have structure in our lives, we are more likely to avoid getting sidetracked by the day's distractions.

Habits can shape our lives, so we must decide what habits we want to create. Our habits can either help us or hold us back. If we want to create the life we desire, we need to be intentional about the habits we form. Daily rituals help us establish the habits that lead to success and keep us moving toward our goals.

Some examples of daily rituals that can improve our lives include meditation, exercise, journaling, and gratitude practices. Meditation helps us calm our minds and reduce stress, while exercise helps us stay healthy and energized. Journaling helps us process our emotions, and gratitude practices help us stay positive and focused on the good things in our lives.

By embracing daily rituals, we take control of our lives and create the foundation for our success. They help us focus on the present, eliminate distractions, and stay on track in achieving our goals. Daily rituals are beneficial and necessary for our well-being and personal growth.

Developing a set of rituals we perform every day is a way to ensure we are making progress toward our goals. When we create daily rituals, we build momentum that carries us forward, and we're more likely to accomplish our goals. Rituals are also an effective way to keep ourselves focused and motivated, especially during challenging times when our willpower and discipline are tested.

Creating daily rituals starts with setting clear goals for ourselves. We must have a clear vision of what we want to accomplish to determine which rituals will help us achieve those goals. The right rituals can help us improve our health, boost our productivity, and deepen our relationships with others.

Developing daily rituals has several benefits. A big one is they help us build habits. Habits are powerful because they shape our lives, and we become what we repeatedly do. Once we develop good habits, they become a part of our daily routine, and we don't even have to think about them. Our brain goes on autopilot, and we become more efficient and effective.

We have many examples of daily rituals that can improve our lives. One habit is journaling. By taking a few minutes daily to reflect on our thoughts and emotions, we can develop a deeper understanding of ourselves and our experiences. I would add another topic to your journaling—gratitude.

Gratitude is a powerful force with the ability to shift our focus and transform our lives. When we take the time to reflect on what we are grateful for, we open ourselves up to a world of possibilities and abundance. When we focus on the positive aspects of our lives, we become more resilient and better equipped to handle life's challenges. Getting caught up in the negative is easy, but when we intentionally seek out the good, we create a buffer against stress and anxiety.

Through journaling, we can train our minds to seek out the good in every situation. Instead of dwelling on what we lack, we can focus on what we have and cultivate gratitude. This, in turn, can help us develop a greater sense of happiness, fulfillment, and purpose.

When we take the time to reflect on our blessings, we also gain a greater appreciation for the people and things in our lives. It's easy to take the good for granted, but when we pause to reflect on what we have, we deepen our connection to the world around us.

In addition to journaling about what I am grateful for, I have also found incorporating other daily rituals into my routine helpful. For example, I make time each day to meditate, which helps me stay centered and calm in the face of stress. I also prioritize daily exercise, which improves my physical health and boosts my mood and energy.

### The Power of Focus

One of the most valuable lessons I have learned is the power of focus. With so many demands on our time and attention, staying present and avoiding distractions can be challenging. However, when we are fully focused on the present moment, we are better able to achieve our goals and experience a deeper sense of fulfillment.

We can use many strategies to stay present and focused, such as setting clear priorities, minimizing distractions, and practicing mindfulness.

One technique that has been particularly effective for me is breaking my day into chunks and dedicating specific periods to different tasks. This allows me to focus entirely on each task without being distracted by other responsibilities.

Another helpful strategy is setting clear goals and objectives. Staying focused and avoiding distractions is easier when we have a clear vision of what we want to achieve.

Finally, staying present and focused requires deep gratitude and appreciation for the present moment. When we are grateful for what we have and fully engaged in the present moment, we can better avoid distractions and focus on our goals.

## Making the Most of What You Have

When we think about achieving our goals, it's easy to get caught up in thinking about what we don't have. If we had more money, more time, more connections, or more resources, we would be able to achieve our dreams. However, the truth is we already have everything we need to start making progress toward our goals. We just need to be resourceful.

Being resourceful means making the most of what we have rather than focusing on what we don't have. It means looking for creative solutions to problems and finding ways to use our resources in new and innovative ways. We can achieve amazing things when we are resourceful, even with limited resources.

A great way to be resourceful is to focus on developing our skills and knowledge. The more we know and develop our skills, the more we can do with the available resources. For example, if you want to start a business but need more money, you can learn about low-cost marketing techniques and how to build a website yourself. These skills can help you get your business off the ground even with limited resources.

Another way to be resourceful is to look for ways to collaborate and connect with others. By building strong relationships and working together, we can pool our resources and achieve more than we could alone. We can share knowledge, expertise, and even physical resources like office space or equipment.

Finally, being resourceful means being willing to take risks and try new things. We often don't have the perfect resources or tools for a given job, but by being open to new ideas and approaches, we usually can find ways to get the job done. Sometimes, taking a calculated risk can be just what we need to break through a difficult challenge and achieve our goals.

When we learn to be resourceful, we can accomplish amazing things. By making the most of what we have, focusing on our skills and knowledge, collaborating with others, and being willing to take risks, we can achieve our goals and thrive in every area of our lives.

## The Role of Hope

Hope is one of the most powerful forces in keeping us going in difficult times. When we face challenges, it's easy to become overwhelmed and lose sight of our goals. But with hope, we can maintain focus and stay on course, no matter how difficult the road ahead may be.

Cultivating hope is a skill that can be learned and strengthened over time. One way to do this is by setting realistic and achievable goals. By breaking down larger goals into smaller, more manageable tasks, we can build a sense of momentum and progress. Celebrating small victories along the way is important because it can help us stay motivated and positive.

Another way to cultivate hope is by surrounding ourselves with supportive and encouraging people. Building a strong network of friends, family, and mentors can help us stay motivated and inspired. It's also important to be a source of hope and inspiration for others because that can help us build strong and lasting relationships.

Finally, keeping a positive mindset and focusing on what we are grateful for is important. By cultivating gratitude and appreciation for the things we have, we can build a sense of hope and optimism that will carry us through even the most challenging times.

In short, hope is essential for success and happiness. We can overcome adversity and achieve our dreams by cultivating hope through achievable goals, supportive relationships, and a positive mindset.

**Self-Reflection**

Are you ready to take the next step in choosing to thrive? As you've learned from this chapter, daily rituals, gratitude journaling, focusing on the present, and cultivating hope are just a few of the powerful tools for navigating adversity and achieving your goals that you have at your disposal. Now, it's time to act. The following questions provoke deep introspection and help you identify patterns that may hold you back. But remember, real progress happens when you take the time to write out your answers and commit to using what you learn to develop integrity and resilience. Take advantage of the opportunity to access new tools and ways of thinking to help you thrive in any circumstance. Answer the questions below and get ready to experience true growth and transformation.

### Questions to Reflect On

- Which daily rituals could you incorporate in your life to help focus on the present and increase your overall well-being?
- When did you last trust your instincts in making an important decision? How did it turn out, and what did you learn from the experience?
- Which people lift you up and help you thrive and who holds you back? What steps can you take to surround yourself with more positive influences?
- How can you maximize the resources available to help you achieve your goals? Are there any untapped opportunities you have yet to explore?
- Which strategies can you use to cultivate hope in difficult times? How can you maintain a positive outlook and stay focused on your goals in the face of adversity?
- How can you use what you learned in this chapter to build up integrity and resilience and face future challenges with

confidence and strength? What specific actions can you take to incorporate these principles into your daily life?

## Summary

- Develop positive daily rituals that align with your goals and values.
- Practice being present in the moment by focusing on your breath, senses, and surroundings.
- Identify and eliminate distractions that prevent you from being fully present and productive.
- Surround yourself with positive, supportive people who lift you up and encourage you to be your best self.
- Cultivate hope by seeking positive experiences and focusing on the opportunities for growth and learning that come with adversity.
- Maximize your resources by being resourceful, creative, and adaptable in facing challenges.

## Conclusion

We have explored the importance of daily rituals, focusing on the present, trusting our instincts, surrounding ourselves with positive people, being resourceful, and cultivating hope in difficult times. These are tools you can use to navigate adversity and achieve your goals. But the most important lesson is: You have the power to choose. You can choose to let life happen to you, or you can choose to take control and create the life you want. It won't always be easy, but it will always be worth it. And when you face challenges in the future, remember the lessons we've discussed and the power of choosing to thrive. You have everything you need within you to overcome any obstacle and create a life of purpose and meaning. So, go forth confidently, and remember the power to thrive is always within you.

# UNLEASHING YOUR OWN POTENTIAL

with Robert Henry

# 8

# THE SCIENCE OF GRATITUDE: HOW POSITIVE EMOTIONS BOOST SUCCESS AND WELL-BEING

*"Gratitude is the healthiest of all human emotions. The more you express gratitude for what you have, the more likely you will have even more to express gratitude for."*

— Zig Ziglar

As I mentioned earlier, my day-to-day began to follow a very specific routine that included meditation, a workout, work, classes, and reading with a focus on increasing my knowledge and understanding, followed by time in the outdoors, whether it was walking the track, tennis, racquetball, or some other recreational activity.

Over time, I became even more grateful for this routine, and I noticed a remarkable change in my attitude toward my situation. Rather than dwelling on the negative aspects of my life, such as the fact that I was in prison, I began to focus on the things I had control over and could be grateful for.

This shift in my mindset took time and effort, but it was necessary. I had to train myself to let go of the things I couldn't control and to focus on what I could. The process required patience, discipline, and self-awareness, but the results were more than worth it.

One of the most significant benefits of this new mindset was that time seemed to fly by when I focused on maximizing my routine. I learned a most valuable lesson about the importance of focusing on the things I could control and the people I associated with.

Speaking of people, I met Geoff during my time in prison. He was also serving time for bank robbery, and we quickly became inseparable. Geoff had a larger-than-life personality and could find humor in any situation, which I found refreshing in the bleak and mundane prison environment.

Geoff had been a bodybuilder before he was incarcerated, and he enjoyed learning racquetball, so our daily schedules quickly intertwined. We spent much time together, laughing, playing pranks, and enjoying life as much as possible in a less-than-ideal situation.

If you've ever watched a movie depicting a military boot camp and seen the scenes with the sleeping quarters, you can pretty much imagine what my "cell" looked like. I lived in a large building that resembled a dormitory, and it housed around 128 inmates.

This dormitory was a long, narrow structure with a hall down the middle. On each side of the hall were eight rooms. The walls dividing the rooms were made of cinderblock and were about six feet tall, while the walls facing the hall were about four feet tall.

Each "room" was a mirror image of one across the hallway. Inside each room were four bunk beds, which meant there were eight inmates living in a single room. In total, there were sixteen rooms in one dormitory. The prison I was in had eight of these identical dormitories.

One day, Geoff came racing around the corner excitedly to tell me something. As he planted himself in a metal folding chair, the entire chair collapsed, leaving him sprawling on the floor. He jumped up to continue his story—the collapsed chair not even phasing him. A couple of minutes later, he suddenly paused, appearing to look for a place to sit, and noticed the ruined metal chair on the floor. He looked so bewildered about the chair that I started laughing nearly uncontrollably.

Of course, that also made him laugh, so we were laughing hysterically as the prison psychologist walked around the corner. Her look of bewilderment made us laugh even more. She planted herself at the entry to our room, and as our laughter finally died down, she asked me a question I will never forget: "Henry, how on earth can you be locked up in prison, yet every time I see you, you look like you're happy and having a great time?"

My answer was a little flippant, but you need to understand I'd taken several personal development classes with the psychologist and even participated with her in a program similar to "Scared Straight," designed to help juveniles get their lives back on track. Our relationship allowed me to get away with jesting with her a bit.

"Well, Doc, that's a great question that I will certainly answer, but in return, you must agree to answer a question of mine."

She hesitated, but her curiosity got the best of her. She agreed.

"Doc, I'm stuck here; no choice in the matter. I did the crime; now I'm doing the time. There are armed guards outside these double fences, topped with wire that could shave a Yeti. So, I'm just trying to make the best of it while I'm here. But tell me, why would a smart, attractive young woman like yourself choose to dive headfirst into this place, surrounded by a bunch of guys who, let's face it, don't always smell like roses?"

The other inmates listening in on our conversation shared a subdued chuckle over my question. The doctor, after a moment's pause, decided to give me a straight answer.

She explained that she came from a financially disadvantaged background. After getting her associate's degree, she realized her passion for psychology. That's when she saw an opportunity: The federal government would foot the bill for her education if she agreed to work for them for a while. It was a savvy move, really. She'd serve her time with the feds and then step into the more lucrative private sector without the weight of crippling student loans dragging her down.

Given that she gave me such an authentic and candid answer, I reciprocated and shared, "Doc, I'm fortunate to have learned a few years ago, in here, to let go of all of the things I have zero control over, and to be grateful for and focus on the things I do have control over. This prison provides me with three hot meals a day. I don't have to worry about where my next meal is coming from. I have a bed to sleep in, no mortgage, and I have access to a gym, a library, a tennis and racquetball court, a baseball field, a basketball court, and I have access to inexpensive college classes. Doc, I could choose to be miserable, and I am sure from living with a hundred criminals in this dorm, which smells like feet and ass, I could find plenty to be miserable about. However, knowing about 70 percent of the world population lives in conditions much worse than this, I choose to focus on what I can be grateful for."

I learned the power of gratitude early in my incarceration, well before it became a popular concept among positive psychology researchers. It became one of the most valuable daily habits I developed in prison. And it wasn't just about being grateful for the basics like food, shelter, and clothing. It was about finding gratitude in every aspect of my life, no matter how small.

It wasn't easy, of course. Some days, I felt hopeless and overwhelmed by my circumstances. But I learned, even in the darkest of times, there was always something to be thankful for. Maybe it was a good book from the library, a workout that left me feeling strong, or a conversation with a fellow inmate that reminded me I wasn't alone.

That sense of camaraderie was especially important to me when I received two letters early in my sentence. One was divorce papers, which I expected, but the other was a letter from my mother saying the family would no longer communicate with me unless I returned to their religion. It was a devastating blow, and I felt like I had no family left.

My friend Geoff saw the look on my face. He knew what the letters said. Without hesitation, he said, "Henry, I'm your family. I'll always be your brother." And he was. Over the next twenty-five years, Geoff remained a constant source of support and friendship, even after his release from prison, eleven months before my release.

Geoff's words resonated with me deeply. I had lost so much, and everything seemed to slip away. But Geoff's friendship showed me I wasn't alone and still had hope. He became my family, closest friend, and support system during one of the toughest times of my life.

As I continued spending time with Geoff, I realized the value of relationships. When you're incarcerated, you're surrounded by hundreds of people, but you quickly learn not all relationships are equal. I saw people come and go. Some left me better than before, while others did not.

The eleven months between Geoff's release and mine were the longest of my incarceration, but they also taught me an important lesson about the value of relationships

I counted myself lucky to have a friend like Geoff in a place as bleak as prison. However, I realized that upon my release, I couldn't leave the fate of my friendships to chance. I needed to be deliberate, seeking out people who shared my values, standards, and a passion for growth and giving back.

Sure, this approach meant I might have fewer friends, but it also meant steering clear of the drama that destructive friendships tend to bring.

Today, I place a high value on meaningful relationships, both personal and professional. I know the people I surround myself with can profoundly influence my happiness, success, and overall well-being. And I'm grateful for every relationship that brings joy, love, and support into my life.

The relationship Geoff and I have has stood the test of time. Even though we live in the same town, we don't cross paths as often as you'd think. Life's gotten busy for him, with his amazing wife Kim and three teenage boys, two of whom face the unique challenges of severe autism. I can't help but feel immense pride in the way he's grown his business, all driven by his unwavering commitment to ensure that his boys have the best care long after he's gone.

In the eyes of my three daughters, Geoff isn't just a friend; he's "Uncle Geoff." They turn to him for guidance, and that fills me with pride and gratitude. His presence in their lives is something I cherish deeply. With grateful tears in my eyes, I share with you that Geoff isn't just a friend; he's family, bound to me for life.

## Gratitude and Positive Emotions

Looking back over those five years in prison, I can confidently say practicing gratitude was one of the most valuable daily habits I developed. It's a simple concept that can profoundly influence your success and well-being.

To introduce the concept of gratitude and positive emotions, I turn to the work of positive psychology researchers like psychologist, educator, and author Martin Seligman and psychologist and UC Davis professor Robert Emmons. Both have studied the effects of gratitude on human behavior and emotions. According to their research, gratitude is a positive emotion that can increase happiness, contentment, and well-being by being thankful for what you have rather than focusing on what you lack.

When you practice gratitude regularly, you're training your brain to focus on the positive aspects of life, which can help you see the world in a more positive light. This positive outlook can have many benefits, including improved relationships, better physical health, and increased resilience when facing challenges.

Regarding gratitude's influence on success and well-being, I turn to the work of authors like Brené Brown and Shawn Achor, who have written extensively about the power of positive emotions. According to such authors, cultivating gratitude can help you achieve your goals by remaining focused on what you want rather than what you fear. When you're grateful for your opportunities and resources, you're more likely to take action to achieve your goals.

Brown argues that gratitude is a key component of resilience, the ability to bounce back from setbacks and challenges. When you're grateful for what you have, you can better cope with adversity and maintain a positive outlook, even when things get tough.

In prison, by focusing on what I had rather than what I lacked, I could cultivate a sense of gratitude that kept me going through some of the darkest times in my life. And ultimately, that gratitude helped me become a more resilient, successful, and fulfilled person.

## The Science of Gratitude

Since my release from prison, in 2004, I have delved deeper into the science behind gratitude and positive emotions, realizing just how powerful this simple practice could be.

Studies have shown that practicing gratitude can profoundly influence our well-being. When we express gratitude, our brains release dopamine and serotonin, neurotransmitters that create feelings of happiness and pleasure. This means even simply thinking about things we are grateful for can boost our mood and create positive neural pathways in the brain.

Researchers have found regularly practicing gratitude can have many physical and psychological benefits. It can reduce symptoms of depression and anxiety, improve sleep quality, increase self-esteem, and even strengthen the immune system.

But how does this work on a neurological level? When we practice gratitude, we activate the brain's reward center, which releases feel-good chemicals like dopamine and serotonin. These chemicals make us feel good at the moment and create positive neural pathways that make it easier to experience positive emotions in the future.

That means the more we practice gratitude, the more our brains are wired to look for the good in situations, even in the midst of challenges and difficulties. And as we train our brains to focus on the positive, we begin to see more opportunities for growth and success.

I can attest to the power of gratitude. During my time in prison, I could have easily focused on the negative aspects of my situation: the cramped living conditions, the limited freedoms, and the constant surveillance. Instead, I chose to focus on what I was grateful for: three hot meals a day, a bed to sleep in, and access to a gym and library.

By focusing on what I had instead of what I lacked, I was able to shift my mindset and find more joy and fulfillment in my daily life. And as I continued to practice gratitude, I became more resilient in the face of challenges and more open to new opportunities for growth and success.

So, if you want to improve your well-being and boost your chances of success, start incorporating gratitude into your daily life. Take time each day to reflect on what you're grateful for—a supportive friend, a beautiful sunset, or a delicious meal. As you practice gratitude more consistently, you'll find your brain begins to rewire itself for positivity and success.

Remember, the power of gratitude lies not just in the momentary pleasure it brings but in the lasting change it can make in our brains and lives.

Another powerful way to cultivate gratitude is through meditation. Meditation allows you to quiet the mind and focus on the present moment, which can help you feel more grateful for the things you have. One simple meditation practice is to sit in a quiet space, close your eyes, and focus on your breath. As you breathe in and out, try to let go of any thoughts or distractions and simply focus on the present moment.

Performing acts of kindness is another technique for cultivating gratitude. When we do things for others, we often feel a sense of gratitude and appreciation for what we have. Acts of kindness can be as simple as holding the door open for someone or giving a compliment, or they can be more involved, like volunteering at a local charity.

Finally, it's important to make gratitude a daily habit. Take time each day to reflect on what you're grateful for, whether through journaling, meditation, or simply taking a few minutes to think about what you appreciate in your life. Making gratitude a habit helps you focus on the positive things in your life, even when things are challenging or difficult.

The science of gratitude shows us that cultivating gratitude is beneficial for our mental and physical health and has a profound influence on our success and well-being. By understanding how gratitude works and practicing techniques for cultivating gratitude, we can begin to rewire our brains for positivity and create more fulfilling and meaningful lives.

## Gratitude's Correlation to Success

As I reflect on gratitude's sway on my journey, I can confidently say the power of gratitude is not to be underestimated. It is not just a simple "thank you" or a fleeting emotion of happiness, but a deep appreciation that can change your entire outlook on life. In this section, I want to explore how gratitude can lead to success in various aspects of our lives.

First, let's talk about how gratitude can boost motivation and productivity. When we focus on what we are grateful for, we naturally shift our attention away from what we lack, which can help us avoid feeling discouraged and negative. Instead, we are more likely to feel energized and motivated to act to achieve our goals. By practicing gratitude regularly, we can develop a positive mindset that fuels us to tackle challenges with purpose and determination. As a result, we become more productive and efficient in our pursuits.

Furthermore, gratitude can also have a profound influence on our relationships and networking opportunities. When we express gratitude toward others, we strengthen our connections with them and foster a sense of trust and goodwill. This can lead to more opportunities for collaboration and support, both in our personal and professional lives. In addition, practicing gratitude can help us cultivate a more empathetic and compassionate approach to communication, making us more effective communicators and leaders.

Unsurprisingly, many successful individuals attribute their achievements to gratitude and positive emotions. Take Oprah Winfrey; she has long advocated for the power of gratitude. She has often spoken about how her daily gratitude practice helped her maintain a positive outlook and attract more abundance.

Another example is former Navy SEAL and author Jocko Willink, who believes that gratitude is essential to mental toughness and resilience. He notes that even in the face of adversity and hardship, we can always find something to be grateful for, which can help us maintain our perspective and motivation.

The science of gratitude is clear: positive emotions can boost our success and well-being in various ways. By cultivating gratitude regularly, making it a habit, we can rewire our brains to focus on the positive and approach challenges with a sense of resilience and determination. Whether in our personal relationships, work, health, or happiness, gratitude can be a powerful tool for achieving success and finding joy.

### Gratitude and Well-Being

One of the most surprising benefits of gratitude is how it can improve physical health and reduce stress. When we experience stress, our bodies release cortisol, a hormone that can cause various negative health effects over time. However, research indicates practicing gratitude can help reduce cortisol levels and improve immune function. One study found participants who wrote down things they were grateful for had less inflammation and improved heart health compared to those who did not practice gratitude.

Gratitude also has a powerful effect on mental health and emotional well-being. When we focus on what we are grateful for, we naturally shift our attention away from negative thoughts and emotions. This shift can help reduce symptoms of depression and anxiety and improve overall emotional well-being. In one study, participants who wrote letters expressing gratitude to someone else experienced a significant improvement in their mood and reported feeling happier and more satisfied with their lives.

I've also seen firsthand how gratitude can help individuals overcome mental health challenges. In prison, I met many people who struggled with addiction, depression, and other mental health issues. However, I noticed those who practiced gratitude regularly were often better able to cope with their challenges and maintain a positive outlook. For example, one friend who struggled with addiction found focusing on gratitude helped him stay motivated and committed to his recovery.

In my own life, cultivating gratitude has been a powerful tool for managing stress and improving my overall health. During my time in prison, I faced countless challenges and difficulties, but by focusing on what I was grateful for, I maintained a sense of optimism and hope.

Gratitude can transform our lives in countless ways, from improving our mental and physical health to enhancing our relationships and boosting our success. By making gratitude a daily practice, we can rewire our brains to focus on the positive aspects of our life, improve our physical and mental health, and build stronger relationships and networks.

## The Power of Perspective

Perspective is a powerful force that shapes our experiences and emotions. The lens through which we view the world can enhance or diminish our well-being. I learned this firsthand while in prison, where I had two choices: focus on the negative aspects of my circumstances or shift my perspective and find gratitude in the midst of adversity.

Here is where the power of gratitude comes into play. Practicing gratitude regularly can shift our perspective and lead to more positive experiences. It allows us to focus on the good in our lives and appreciate the small things we often take for granted. By acknowledging and expressing gratitude for the positive aspects of our lives, we can train our brains to focus on the good and see the world in a more positive light.

One study found that individuals who practiced gratitude regularly experienced a 23 percent reduction in cortisol, the stress hormone, and a 10 percent increase in overall happiness. This research supports the idea that cultivating gratitude can have significant physical and mental health benefits.

Gratitude also helps us recognize and appreciate the people and experiences in our lives. Expressing gratitude to those around us strengthens our relationships and creates a more positive environment. Gratitude can enhance our social connections and give us a sense of community and belonging.

In my personal experience, I have found that gratitude can transform our lives. It has allowed me to shift my perspective, find joy in the present moment, and cultivate positive relationships with those around me.

Perspective is a powerful force that shapes our experiences and emotions. By cultivating gratitude and shifting our perspective, we can enhance our well-being, improve our relationships, and experience more positive emotions. Gratitude has the power to transform our lives, so it is a habit we should all regularly strive to cultivate.

## Self-Reflection

As you come to the end of this chapter on the science of gratitude and its effect on success and well-being, take a moment to reflect on the insights and lessons you learned. While reading this chapter has been informative, the real progress comes when you take the time to apply these principles to your own life. So, I invite you to write out your answers to the following questions.

## Questions to Reflect On

- How can you cultivate a daily gratitude practice, and how will it improve your overall well-being?
- How has your perspective on past challenges changed after learning about the science of gratitude?
- Can you recall a time when shifting your perspective to gratitude could have helped you overcome a challenging

situation? How might you handle a similar situation differently in the future with a grateful perspective?

- How can you actively practice gratitude in your relationships with others and improve your connections with those around you?
- How can you integrate gratitude into your daily routine to increase motivation, productivity, and success in your personal and professional life?
- How might you inspire and encourage others to cultivate a daily gratitude practice and share the benefits of positive emotions with those around you?
- Which three things are you grateful for right now? Write it as if future generations might read this, and you want them to be inspired by what you write.

**Summary**

- Practice gratitude regularly to rewire your brain for positivity.
- Cultivate gratitude through techniques like journaling, meditation, and actively seeking out things to be grateful for.
- Make gratitude a habit by incorporating it into your daily routine.
- Use the power of gratitude to increase motivation, productivity, and success in various areas of your life.

- Improve your relationships and networking opportunities by expressing gratitude toward others.
- Use gratitude to improve your physical and mental health, reduce stress, and increase emotional well-being.

## Conclusion

I hope you have gained a newfound appreciation for the beauty and abundance surrounding you. Remember every moment is a gift, and it is up to you to find joy in the simple things. By focusing on the positive, you can create a ripple effect that enhances your own life and the lives of those around you. Take a moment to reflect on all your blessings and feel gratitude for all you have been given. Remember, even in the midst of adversity, there is always something to be grateful for. By cultivating a grateful heart and practicing gratitude regularly, you can unlock the power of positive emotions, the key to success and well-being. Remember, life is a journey, and gratitude is the compass guiding you to a brighter future.

# UNLEASHING YOUR OWN POTENTIAL

with Robert Henry

# 9

# BUILDING A SUPPORT SYSTEM: THE ROLE OF RELATIONSHIPS IN PERSONAL GROWTH AND SUCCESS

*"I'm a success today because I had a friend who believed in me and I didn't have the heart to let him down. It's in our relationships where we find the courage to grow."*

— Abraham Lincoln

In the summer of 2003, the chain-link fences and razor-wire curls of the Federal Correctional Institution in Safford, Arizona, which had defined my world for five grueling years, were to become a distant specter. A chapter of life tattooed with remorse and regret was nearing its conclusion. As my sentence ticked down to the final days, the last vestiges of imprisonment were about to slip from my being like discarded skin. But in that impending transition lay the seeds of a daunting question: Could I truly leave behind the memories of incarceration? Would the world accept me not as a former inmate but a man seeking redemption?

Imprisonment is a duality of existence. While the body is confined within the correctional system's high walls and stark regimentation, the mind is left to roam free. Those solitary hours within my cell were a crucible, forging me into a new man. Like an alchemist, I had stirred together the remorse of my past, the stoicism of my present, and my nebulous hope for the future into a transformative elixir. This concoction was my survival mechanism; it allowed me to envision a life beyond the cold bars and impersonal uniforms.

San Diego had always resonated with me; its energy seemed to pulse with a rhythm that matched my heartbeat. In an attempt to bridge the chasm between my confined existence and the throbbing life of the city, I subscribed to a local newspaper. It became my tether to the outside world, offering tantalizing glimpses of normalcy and a sense of belonging. Every column, every word was a window that brought me closer to the rhythm of life in San Diego, to the cadence of freedom.

Buoyed by optimism, I dared to reach out to potential employers in San Diego. In missive after missive, I laid bare my past, present incarceration, and earnest intentions for the future. Like messages in a bottle, I cast them into the vast sea of societal judgment, pinning my hopes on the kindness of strangers. It was an act of vulnerability, of risking rejection. But in my heart, I knew it was a gamble I had to take.

Amid the daily hustle of San Diego's construction industry, my plea found an echo. An invitation arrived, a chance for redemption. The offer of employment became the beacon that would guide me through the uncharted waters of post-prison life. I had stepped into the realm of possibilities; the high walls and the omnipresent guards could no longer restrict my spirit.

Emancipation was a bittersweet paradox. I was free, yet I carried the weight of my past. I was at the threshold of a world I had left behind five years earlier, yet I knew it had moved on without me. The society I was about to reenter had continued its rhythm undisturbed by my absence. Could I synchronize my beat with its pulse? Would the world accept the melody of a man who had once strayed from its harmony?

But in my heart, I knew my past was a tale already told, and my future was yet to be determined. I was ready to write a new chapter, not as a man shackled by guilt and regret, but as a man reaching out for redemption, ready to contribute and thrive. The chain-link fences and the razor wire, once symbols of my confinement, were now the gateway to my resurrection.

The days leading up to my release and the day itself felt like a dream, something not quite real. My time was spent in isolation, walking around the track, lost in my thoughts, whenever I wasn't working, eating, or sleeping. I chose solitude to avoid any possible conflicts with fellow inmates. On my last night, I walked by the fence and thought, *Right now, touching this fence could get me shot. But in less than twelve hours, I'll walk out of here a free man.* It was a strange realization: one moment, I was seen as a threat to society; the next, I was deemed harmless. My mind struggled to wrap around this transition.

Admittedly, I felt a mix of excitement and fear. Prison life, with its predictability, provided a sense of security. I had daily routines, guaranteed meals, a place to sleep, and familiar faces all around. My time at FCI Safford had even earned me a certain level of respect from both guards and inmates. But stepping back into the "real world" was stepping into the unknown. Despite the uncertainty, I was ready to turn the page and start anew.

Then came the day of my release. At 4:30 a.m., on Monday, August 25, 2003, I, Inmate 54232-198, Robert W. Henry, was walked from my dorm to the Administrative Office. There, I was given shoes, jeans, a shirt, $100, and a plane ticket voucher for a flight from Phoenix to San Diego.

A correctional officer met me outside the prison, and we drove three-and-a-half hours to the Phoenix Airport. Once there, he simply wished me luck and left. For the first time in five years, I traveled without handcuffs, finally on my way to a new chapter in life, full of possibilities and freedom.

Stepping into the bustling Phoenix Airport was a stark contrast to my years of confinement—it was overwhelming and exhilarating all at once. For the first time in a long while, I was alone, surrounded by the public, and no longer under the watchful eye of law enforcement. I made my way to the ticket counter, ready to exchange my voucher for a real plane ticket.

In the crowded airport, people jostled past me, some even bumping into me without a second glance. This brusque behavior took me aback; in prison, even the smallest bump would be met with a quick apology. After all, you never knew what might be going on in someone else's life—a misplaced bump could be the catalyst for a much larger conflict.

The airport was a sensory overload. Bright colors and noisy crowds were a far cry from the muted tones and structured routine of prison life. My anxiety began to mount as I navigated this new, chaotic environment.

When I reached the counter, the ticket agent asked for my ID. I hesitantly handed over my Bureau of Prisons ID Card, its "INMATE" label and my inmate number glaringly obvious. The agent glanced at it briefly before offering, "Mr. Henry, your reservation is for 1:00 p.m., but we have a seat available on a flight leaving in forty minutes. Would you like to take that one instead?"

A surge of panic and indecision washed over me. *Is this a trap? Are they testing me?* I wondered, lost in my thoughts until the agent gently prompted, "Sir?"

Snapping back to reality, I agreed to the earlier flight, thinking it would give me a chance to enjoy a leisurely breakfast at a real restaurant before I had to report to the halfway house. According to the terms of my release, I was on "furlough" and required to check into the halfway house by 3:00 p.m. Failure to do so would label me as an escapee, putting me on the U.S. Marshals' radar and potentially adding another five years to my sentence. I knew I couldn't afford to take any chances.

Upon my arrival in San Diego, breakfast at Denny's felt like a feast, the metallic clang of real cutlery against porcelain plates a symphony of freedom. It was euphoria, sensory overload, an awakening from the dull monotony of prison life. The taste of scrambled eggs, the feel of a cotton napkin, the sight of people immersed in the throes of their daily routines, each moment was a celebration of freedom.

Upon my release, I found myself navigating a new chapter in a halfway house, situated right in the heart of Barrio Logan—one of San Diego's most notorious neighborhoods, known for its tumultuous gang activity. This halfway house was uniquely positioned on the volatile turf boundary of the Crips and the Bloods, rival gangs with a storied history of conflict.

My first month was marked by a strict routine: heading off to work during the day and promptly returning to the halfway house each evening. This facility, while reminiscent of the prison I had just left, had its differences, notably the presence of both men and women, though our living quarters were distinctly separated. The halfway house had communal areas for dining, recreational spaces, and outdoor areas for some much-needed fresh air.

I had initially decided to keep to myself, avoiding forming any connections in this transitional space. However, it wasn't long before I found camaraderie with Mike, a local surfer and fellow resident, with whom I shared workouts, and Jodi, a young woman also residing there for minor offenses. In this unique environment, I unexpectedly found myself regarded as something of an "Original Gangster" due to the nature of my past crime.

To maximize my time outside these facilities, I juggled two jobs—one in construction during the day and another in janitorial work in the evenings. My goal was clear: to immerse myself as much as possible in the outside world, creating a distance from the halfway house, while navigating this critical transition back into society.

Embracing my newfound liberty, I plunged headlong into my work, honing my craft in the construction industry. I savored the earthy smell of timber, the rhythmic thud of a hammer against a nail, and the artistic precision of blueprints. I reveled in the camaraderie of my colleagues; each brick we laid, every wall we erected, was a testament to our collective endeavor, a symbol of my personal and professional rebuilding.

In the relative normalcy of work, I found a haven from the prejudiced whispers of society. Yet, the curious gazes and the hushed speculations about my past were inescapable. Could I step out of the shadow of my past? Should I bare my history to those around me or shroud it in silence? In the face of their unasked questions, I made a decision that would become my creed—to be honest with myself and others.

The revelation came during an impromptu gathering at a café after a volleyball game. Amid the clatter of coffee cups and the buzzing chatter, I found myself at the center of the team's curiosity. Their questions tumbled out in a cascade, probing my past. With a deep breath and a steadying sip of coffee, I embraced transparency. I pulled out my Department of Justice Inmate photo ID card and set it on the table, a tangible testament to my past.

The café fell silent and then erupted in a wave of disbelief. Their wide-eyed stares met the undeniable truth. I was a convict, a man bearing the scars of his mistakes. While initially shocking, the revelation broke the barriers of our acquaintance, fostering a deeper connection. Their curiosity transformed into empathy, their disbelief into understanding. I became an open book, a tale of a fall and redemption, an account of lessons learned within the high walls of a prison.

As I recounted the moments of my incarceration, the gritty realities, and the fleeting moments of levity, I became a storyteller. I was no longer an ex-convict but a man who had learned life's hardest lessons. As I unveiled the layers of my past, many reciprocated with tales of their mistakes, their regrets, and their yearnings for redemption. It was as if my honesty had unlocked a trove of confessions, weaving a tapestry of human frailty and resilience.

The experience was an epiphany, a realization that every life is a story, each with its chapters of triumphs and tribulation. In our shared vulnerabilities, I saw an opportunity, an opportunity to transform my life's story into a beacon for others, a tale that could guide others through their darkest times.

And thus, in a bustling café in San Diego, amid the hum of conversations and the clatter of coffee cups, I found a purpose. I would write a book. I would use my story not as a tale of regret but as a testament to redemption, a guide for those seeking a path out of their mistakes. It was my chance to contribute, to turn my past into a beacon for others. The transition was complete from inmate to storyteller, from convict to beacon of hope.

Life, however, had another surprise waiting for me. Among the people I met playing volleyball was Donna, a dental hygienist and an aspiring real estate investor. Her vivacious spirit and goal-driven outlook struck a chord with me. Our friendship blossomed amid shared dreams and volleyball games, developing into a romantic relationship.

As our relationship evolved, Donna offered me an opportunity to partner with her in a real estate investment. It was a chance to use my skills in the construction industry, a step toward fulfilling my entrepreneurial dreams. We struck a deal; she would fund the materials, and I would invest my time and skills to renovate a house.

The project tested my resilience and determination, a trial by fire. Each day presented its own set of challenges, from sourcing the right materials to managing subcontractors. But the thrill of seeing the house transform, brick by brick, wall by wall under my artistry was intoxicating. It was an empowering experience, a validation of my skills and potential.

Completing the project marked a turning point. The dated property had morphed into a beautiful home, a manifestation of my and Donna's shared vision. We sold the house for a substantial profit, marking our first successful venture. The excitement of the venture sparked a passion in me, a desire to carve my niche in construction and real estate.

As I revelled in our venture's success, I received a surprising offer. The owner of the construction company I was working for offered me a promotion to supervisor. It was a moment of validation, a recognition of my skills and leadership abilities.

But the offer was also a dilemma. Accepting the promotion meant getting entrenched in the comfort of a salaried job, a secure routine. To decline would mean venturing into the uncertainty of entrepreneurship, the excitement of shaping my destiny. I remembered a professor from my prison days telling me that when I was promoted to supervisor, it was time to venture out on my own.

So, I decided to decline the offer, choosing entrepreneurship. As I handed in my two weeks' notice, I could see the surprise in the owner's eyes. But he wished me well, acknowledging my desire to shape my own path.

As I started this new chapter of my life, I got another surprising piece of news. Donna was pregnant. The news brought a wave of emotions. I was elated by the prospect of becoming a father—but also anxious about whether I was ready to be a good one.

To add fuel to this whirlwind of emotions, we realized San Diego might not be the best environment to raise our child. We yearned for a more peaceful setting, a smaller community that could offer a nurturing environment. We chose to move to Spokane, Washington, a city promising the tranquility of nature and the convenience of urban amenities.

And so, we embarked on our journey to Spokane. Our daughter Olivia was born as we settled into our new home, ushering in a new chapter in our lives. The moment I held her in my arms, I felt an overwhelming wave of love and protective instinct. I was a father, responsible for a life, and committed to shaping a future.

My journey into fatherhood coincided with my venture into entrepreneurship. As I nurtured Olivia, I nurtured my dream of building a successful construction company. In the pursuit of my dreams, I met Greg, a neighbor who was a successful business owner.

Greg and I hit it off instantly. We shared common interests, from weekend trips to the lake to racquetball games. Our friendship deepened over time, fostering a sense of camaraderie and mutual respect. Greg's entrepreneurial journey became an inspiration for me, a blueprint of success.

One Christmas, Greg gave me an iPod. It wasn't the device itself but the content it held that became a life-changing gift. The iPod was filled with audiobooks by personal development gurus like Brian Tracy, Zig Ziglar, and Norman Vincent Peale. Each book was a lesson in self-improvement, a guide to personal and professional growth.

My morning runs became an opportunity to absorb these lessons. As I pounded the pavement, the words of these masters resonated within me, kindling a spark of inspiration. I realized the power of personal development, the potential to transform oneself through knowledge and action.

The iPod was one of the greatest and most profound gifts anyone had ever given me. And it would help me face my next greatest setback since prison…but that story is for the next chapter.

## Reflecting on the Importance of Relationships in Personal Growth and Success

Life is a journey, a complex web of interactions and experiences, and every step we take shapes us in ways we could never fully comprehend. My journey took a unique and challenging detour. A period of my life was spent in a prison's cold, hard surroundings and the transitional pathway of a halfway house. This chapter of my life, filled with stark contrasts and heavy lessons, taught me one crucial, unyielding truth—relationships, in every form and every space, hold the power to shape us profoundly.

In the heart of solitude, among the uniformity of prison life, I came to understand the words of Brené Brown when she said, "Connection is why we're here; it's what gives purpose and meaning to our lives." The relationships I built within those austere walls with individuals from all walks of life, each with their unique stories, broke the monotony, lighting up the grayness with shades of understanding, empathy, and shared resilience.

Whether it was an unlikely friendship with a fellow inmate, a quietly respectful relationship with a guard, or even the limited but crucial connection with the outside world via occasional visitors, each bond carved a semblance of normalcy into the abnormal. And, surprisingly, these relationships taught me about the power of honesty, of owning one's mistakes, and of redemption.

Yet, it was transitioning to the halfway house that made the true magnitude of relationships in the path to recovery and personal growth starkly evident. Like the halfway house standing at the crossroads between prison and freedom, relationships too were junctions—of past experiences, present realities, and future hopes.

In the halfway house, I learned in life, like in volleyball, the key is not to avoid the ball (or experiences, in a broader sense) but to volley with purpose, dexterity, and collaboration. Relationships built on the court, around shared interests, connected me back to society and reminded me of a time before the prison walls when I was not an inmate but a human being, full of dreams, hopes, and potential.

Echoing the words of Stephen Covey, "Interdependence is a higher value than independence." In the world outside the prison, where I strived to reclaim my identity, my relationships became my guiding North Star, leading me toward growth and away from past mistakes. In sharing my story with others, I was surprised to find acceptance and relatability rather than judgment. It reminded me that we are, at our core, imperfectly human, molded by our errors and redeemed by our desire to learn and grow from them.

So, the life lesson I offer you, drawn from personal experience and the shared wisdom of personal development experts, is: Never underestimate the power of relationships. Whether on a high mountain peak or in a deep valley, the connections you foster can guide, uplift, and fundamentally change you. Embrace these relationships, for they are the true architects of personal growth and success.

Life is not a solitary journey. It's an intricate dance of connections, a shared story written together with the people we meet, the bonds we build, and the relationships we cherish. And so we grow, not alone but together, in the communal narrative of life, learning, and love.

### Choosing Your Network Wisely

Choosing our friends wisely is one of the most pivotal decisions we can make. As Jim Rohn said, "You are the average of the five people you spend the most time with." Here are a four tips to navigate this choice.

1. Identify individuals who embody the values you hold dear. These could be honesty, kindness, resilience, ambition, or any trait you deeply resonate with.
2. Consider how these potential friends respond in a crisis or difficulty. Friends who stick by you, offer support, and inspire you to rise above challenges are the ones to keep.
3. Be mindful of how you feel around them. Do you feel uplifted, inspired, and accepted for who you are? Do you feel encouraged to grow, to improve? If yes, these are signs of a healthy friendship.
4. Remember that friendships should be reciprocal. It's not only about what you can get but also about what you can give. Friendships provide us with a platform to receive support and love and give it back in abundance.

To sum up, choose friends who align with your values, support you during challenges, inspire personal growth, and encourage reciprocity.

## Self-Reflection

As you journey through these pages, it's vital to remember the real transformation isn't in the reading but in the doing. The questions below are designed to provoke deep self-reflection to initiate pattern changes that will serve as your compass during future adversities.

The potential for growth lies in your hands, in your willingness to delve into these questions, answer them sincerely, and apply what you learn to your life. As you write out your responses, think of each word as a step toward developing a greater sense of integrity, a powerful tool that will guide you when you face adversity. Remember, true progress isn't marked by knowledge acquisition but by its application. So, let's dive deeply into the realm of self-reflection, knowing that within it lies the key to unlocking our best selves.

## Questions to Reflect On

- Reflecting on your past experiences, can you identify a moment when adversity pushed you to develop new ways of thinking or behaving? How did that moment reshape your approach to life's challenges?
- What role have your relationships played in shaping the person you are today? Can you pinpoint certain individuals who have

had a significant positive or negative influence on your life's trajectory?

- How has your choice of friends and associates influenced your life, goals, and the way you handle adversity? If you were to be more intentional in choosing your circle, what qualities would you look for?

- How have you applied the principle of integrity? Can you share a specific instance when staying true to your values helped you overcome a difficult situation?

- Based on what you've learned in this chapter, how would you rewrite your approach to adversity? How can you better use your relationships, integrity, and personal growth tools to navigate future challenges?

- Looking forward, how do you plan to integrate these insights into your everyday life? How might your personal and professional relationships be influenced by the changes you intend to make?

## Summary

- **Evaluate Your Circle:** Be intentional about whom you allow into your life. Surround yourself with individuals who inspire you, support your growth, and positively contribute to your journey. Evaluate the people in your life and make sure they align with your values and aspirations.

- **Cultivate Positive Relationships:** Take an active role in building relationships. Remember that genuine, positive relationships are a two-way street—they require mutual respect, understanding, and investment.

- **Foster Integrity:** Live a life consistent with your values and beliefs. This means always being honest, not only with others but more importantly with yourself. Your integrity will serve as a solid foundation in your personal growth journey.

- **Leverage Your Support System:** Use the support of your relationships to navigate life's challenges and adversities. Remember, it's not a sign of weakness to lean on your support system when times get tough; rather, it's a testament to your strength and resilience.

- **Continual Learning:** Always be open to learning and growth. This includes learning from your experiences, relationships, and even your mistakes. Treat every experience as an opportunity to learn and develop as a person.

- **Apply Lessons Learned:** It's one thing to learn a lesson; it's another to apply what you've learned to your life. Take the insights you've gained from your experiences and actively work to apply them in your everyday life, especially when facing adversity.

## Conclusion

Whether it's navigating the stark walls of a prison, the hustle of a halfway house, or the newfound freedoms of independent life, these moments uncover our deepest reserves of resilience and determination.

Choosing the right company, those individuals who inspire us and challenge us, is a journey in itself. Yet it's a journey worth taking because these relationships play a pivotal role in our growth, pushing us to be better, do better, and strive for more. Through these connections, we find a mirror held up to our true selves, nudging us toward honesty, integrity, and authenticity.

Being open to personal development, whether through an iPod loaded with the wisdom of legends or through quiet moments of introspection, illuminates the path toward our true potential. A unique kind of empowerment is found in embracing continuous learning and knowing you hold the key to your own transformation. With each lesson learned and applied, we are not merely surviving our adversities but thriving despite them.

And finally, as you go forth on your own journey, remember to show yourself grace. Know it's okay to make mistakes, to falter, and to fall and fail. But it's equally important to rise, to learn, and to grow from these experiences. You are the architect of your life, the author of your story. Make it a masterpiece.

The journey may be fraught with challenges, but with every step you take, with every relationship you nurture, with every lesson you learn, remember you are growing, evolving, and becoming the person you were always meant to be. And that, my friend, is the most beautiful journey of all.

# UNLEASHING YOUR OWN POTENTIAL

*with Robert Henry*

# 10

# OVERCOMING ADVERSITY: ALL JOURNEYS WILL ENTAIL SETBACKS

*"I am not concerned that you have fallen—I am concerned that you arise."*

— Abraham Lincoln

My life was headed in my chosen direction, and I was making great progress! I lived in an amazing, brand-new home Donna and I had purchased in a new development. We brought our daughter home from the hospital to a beautiful nursery Donna had created. My heart brimmed with gratitude and excitement about the future.

We made friends quickly in our new city and had great neighbors. The future looked bright!

I'd started my construction company, and since I was in the construction boom of 2004 to 2007, my business took off. I started doing remodels and soon did large projects for local celebrities. I became a regular on several local news channels for participating in heartfelt construction projects supporting less fortunate community members encountering difficulties.

Learning to balance a construction company with twenty-eight employees simultaneously working on a dozen projects while figuring out the intricacies of raising a baby girl was challenging, but I was eager to do well. In prison, I'd set a standard for myself to be the best I could be in any role I took on.

I had a ten-year plan to become the biggest residential construction company in the area and then sell it. In 2008, the market collapsed around me. I'd been so focused on growth I had paid little attention to the media. I also didn't understand financial or economic cycles. I was woefully unprepared to handle the real estate collapse.

Suddenly, I had major projects underway that I could not continue the payments on. Simultaneously, millions of dollars in signed contracts scheduled to begin that year were canceled due to market instability. We went from having eighteen projects under construction to four.

I had to start laying off employees, which was one of the toughest things I'd had to do. We had a reputation for having great people and being a great employer—again, remember the standard I'd set for myself. If I were going to be an employer, I would be the best employer I could possibly be.

By early 2008, we were down to only four employees. I resolved to do my best to ride out the recession. I'd burned through more than $300,000 from our personal savings to keep suppliers and subcontractors paid. We took on jobs where we were certainly one of the lowest bidders to keep my people working and make some progress.

Then, the owners refused to pay their final bill on two projects we were completing. I was devastated. I couldn't afford to pay attorneys to place liens on the homes, and I think the owners must have known they were protecting their capital at the start of what would be a deep recession.

At that point, I'd exhausted our savings, bills were stacking up, and I couldn't make payroll. I was scared.

I spoke with an attorney client of mine and my insurance company seeking advice. "Shut it down—immediately." I could not fathom quitting. There had to be another way.

"If the economy suddenly turned around today, it would take you a minimum of five and more likely seven years to break even."

They advised me to shut down the company that week and file for bankruptcy to protect the only thing we had left, the home we were raising our daughter in. At that point, we had two major projects we were in the middle of. I did my best to ensure those clients were made whole—that they'd only paid for the work actually completed. I even tried to hand them off to another contractor I'd worked with who agreed to take on the projects and honor the pricing and timelines we'd initially agreed to.

Nevertheless, the clients were angry. They didn't understand. Shutting down the company felt like the ultimate betrayal of their trust. I didn't blame them; surely, I would have felt the same way.

It was an awful time. I was as embarrassed about my failure as I was for being a bank robber. Was I just a failure?

I confided in my friend and neighbor Greg, who had given me the iPod full of books. Since he'd started and successfully sold several companies, I really valued his input.

He said an entrepreneur learns the most from their failures. Nearly everyone succeeds in a great economy. What you do when the economy kicks you in the teeth is the measure of how you'll ultimately succeed.

Well, it was too late for my construction company; however, I began searching for what I could have done to be better prepared for an economic downturn. I once again began studying. I studied economic cycles, cash flow, the building industry, and housing cycles.

I transitioned into a career in real estate and threw myself into learning the trade.

Again, life threw a devastating curveball. Our six-year-old daughter, Olivia, developed an intensely aggressive autoimmune disease that was difficult to diagnose. She began losing weight alarmingly. She was admitted to intensive care and spent five months fighting for her life.

After months of tests, procedures, and surgeries, they finally made a diagnosis and began helping her treat the symptoms.

The process was heart-wrenching, stressful, and very expensive. At one point, we just quit thinking about the costs—we could worry about that when she finally started improving.

Soon after finally bringing our daughter home, Donna informed me she no longer wished to be married in the institution's traditional sense. She wanted to be co-parents and friends.

Our journey together had been anything but smooth, filled with tumultuous challenges and unforeseen hardships. The closure of our business, accompanied by the daunting specter of bankruptcy, had left us reeling, and the subsequent loss of our home to foreclosure only deepened our distress. Amid this chaos, the near-loss of our cherished daughter pushed us to our limits. Under the weight of these trials, Donna's faith in my capacity to support and be the partner she needed began to waver.

The relentless series of setbacks had understandably eroded Donna's confidence, casting shadows of doubt on my ability to navigate us through these stormy times. Through it all, I saw the strain in her eyes, the silent questions about our future, and my role in it. In the face of these adversities, Donna's belief in me was tested, and her assurance in my role as her husband was shaken. Once again, I felt deflated. I wanted my daughter to grow up in a two-parent family. This change would go against what I wanted and valued most.

I had just started my career in real estate as a new agent and was torn between launching a very demanding career, in which two out of three agents fail within the first three years, and trying to figure out how to save my marriage.

Over the course of the next two years, I attended countless seminars on personal growth, relationships, marriage, parenting, leadership, coaching, etc.

Through all of that, I realized something about our marriage. I would have to have a major breakthrough in making my wife feel emotionally safe in our relationship and have the independence she craved at the same time—an elegant dance I could not master sufficiently to make a difference in our marriage in time.

Donna had grown up in a household with a very demanding and somewhat controlling father. I realized much later, after we separated, that so many things about marriage represented "control" for her, subconsciously causing her to resent the "controls" or limitations marriage represented in her mind.

That underlying resistance to control left Donna focused on anything her mind deemed controlling, and in her mind, nearly everything felt like it encroached on her independence.

I was beginning to get some traction with my real estate career, so our company's CEO suggested I start mentoring agents and teaching classes. "You'll be great at it, and furthermore, you will become addicted to contributing to other people."

He was right. I loved it. So much so that today, many years later, much of my daily life involves public speaking, teaching seminars, and coaching. However, it nearly didn't go in that direction.

One agent I was particularly fond of had a similar experience being a builder during the recession in 2007-2008. He transitioned into real estate in 2010, and I mentored him, showing him the ropes. We were two months into our training together, and while I realized he was grappling with depression over losing his business, I was in no way prepared when his wife called the day after he missed his coaching appointment.

"Russ took his life yesterday," she said.

I'll never forget how I felt hearing those words. I felt like the breath had been knocked out of me. I don't even remember what I said. What can you say?

I was disappointed, hurt, sad, and angry all at once. I stewed for hours before calling one of my personal development coaches.

"Jo, I cannot be the kind of person who doesn't recognize that someone I 'know' is suffering to the extent that the only viable relief they see is to take their own life. How could I be so blind?" I asked. I resolved, "I will *not* achieve success in my own life without bringing people along with me. I want to make a difference in people's lives, Jo! I want to help people I interact with become the best versions of themselves, for themselves, their families, their friends, and their future. And it is too important to fuck it up or dabble with…. It's people's lives. Where do I start?"

She encouraged me to take a seven-month intensive course on leadership. "It's a grueling, intense, and demanding course. Only two in ten successfully complete it and graduate."

I didn't even hesitate. I signed up. At the time, it represented the biggest financial investment in my own training. Spending thirty hours a week in classrooms, doing homework, breakout sessions, and attending multiple weekend seminar sessions in other cities was a huge commitment.

I was excited. The program's founders also teach leadership courses at Harvard, and elements of the program are taught at West Point. Upon graduation, they offered a program where I could train to be an elite business coach for corporations and businesses worldwide.

From day one of the program, I struggled with getting all of the program requirements on my calendar. "Wow, this is a lot! What the heck did I agree to?"

A young woman named Cambria, who appeared to be twelve (she was actually twenty-seven), walked over and said, "What are you grappling with right now."

I sized her up as being way too young to know what she was talking about and dismissively said, "This program is a massive commitment. I don't know about these other participants, but I have a life and commitments outside of my already demanding career that I'm not sure I want to sacrifice."

Cambria had recently graduated from the same program. She was there to assist in getting all the participants up to speed.

"I'm curious what interested you in the program to begin with?" she replied.

I briefly told her my story—perhaps a bit begrudgingly. Cambria might have only looked twelve, but it was a pretty ingenious question to redirect my thinking. When I finished, she said, "It sounds like you are looking at the *entire* seven-month program as one big chunk. Let's just look at the requirements and dates listed and then put them into your calendar one week at a time, making sure we also block out the activities crucial to your business and personal life."

Shit. I couldn't come up with an excuse. She sauntered away, probably a little pleased with herself.

*Well, heck,* I thought, *if that's the kind of coaching I can get in this program, even if it is from a twelve-year-old, this is going to be great.*

In seven months, I never saw or heard from her again. It didn't matter. The program was intense. We learned how to listen to what people *were not saying*, help them discover for themselves what matters most to them, and become a trusted advocate for others in realizing their full potential. It was exactly what I was looking for.

Sure enough, only a few of us graduated, myself included. It was one of the most transformational periods of my life. I'm still close to the instructor, Laurie, and will be forever grateful for the massive contribution her training has made to my life. I made several friends in that program. As the years have flown by, my friendship with Alvera and Jessica evolved into something far deeper. They are more than just friends I met along the way; they are the sisters my heart chose. Time has only strengthened our bond, keeping it as vibrant and steadfast as when our paths first crossed.

After graduating, I received a call that changed my life forever.

The twelve-year-old called—okay, I'll stop calling her that, but to this day, Cambria still looks fifteen years younger than her actual age, and well, she also happens to be the same height as the average twelve-year-old!

Cambria called to ask if I'd like to set up being each other's daily accountability coach.

We had both been trained to become elite performance coaches by one of the top coaching companies in the world. Cambria suggested we practice with each other as accountability coaches via a daily call.

In a nutshell, an accountability coach helps clients set and achieve personal or professional goals by keeping them accountable. They provide guidance, support, encouragement, and constant motivation to ensure their clients stay on track. An accountability coach's responsibilities include:

- **Goal Setting:** Helping clients establish clear, realistic, and achievable goals.
- **Planning:** Assisting clients in creating a strategic action plan to reach their goals.
- **Monitoring:** Keeping track of clients' progress toward their goals, often through regular check-ins, in our case, daily.
- **Motivation:** Providing encouragement and support to keep clients motivated and focused, especially when they feel discouraged or distracted. This is tricky and requires a deep understanding of what a client most needs to remain motivated.
- **Feedback:** Offering constructive feedback and alternative strategies when obstacles or setbacks come up.
- **Accountability:** Holding clients responsible for their actions and decisions to ensure they stay committed to their path and make consistent progress toward their goals.

Accountability coaches can work in various areas, such as fitness, nutrition, business, and personal growth. The main idea is to have someone hold you accountable for the commitments you've made to yourself, keeping you motivated and on track.

Cambria and I had a daily call at 5:00 a.m. for nearly two years. During our calls, we talked about what we accomplished or didn't accomplish from the previous day's agenda and commitments. We shared what we allowed to get in the way of achieving our commitments the previous day. No excuses, no bullshit. Just total authenticity. It taught me to focus on what mattered most to me and honor commitments to the highest degree ever.

I was pleased with the direction my career, coaching endeavors, and life were going. I was helping more and more people, really making a difference, and my real estate career was doing well.

During that time, I continued my leadership training by coaching participants of the next leadership program. I was eventually invited to be the head coach for the program, coaching the coaches!

Then, in early 2012, two things happened that changed the course of our separate trajectories. I needed to recruit coaches for the next program when I became a head coach. I asked Cambria. She agreed.

We started traveling to the same events and seeing each other several times a week. She also decided that in addition to her recruiting/head-hunting company, she'd get her real estate license.

"Hey, guess what?" she said one day when she called me. "I'm walking into the testing office to take my real estate exam."

What? I had not expected that.

She completed her exam and waltzed into my office, announcing we were now working together.

Cambria went on a trip, and I agreed to pick her up at the airport when she returned. While sitting in the car waiting for her, I had this realization: "Oh crap, I'm in love with my best friend. I will ruin one of the best relationships I've ever had because I let myself fall in love." When Cambria got in the car, she looked at my face and said, "So, what are you grappling with right now?"

Sound familiar?

"It just hit me," I said. "I'm in love with you. And you're the best friend I could possibly want. I'm scared being in love with you will screw up something so great. I don't know what to do."

She was quiet for way longer than I was comfortable with, leaving my mind and heart racing.

Finally, she said, "Yeah. I'm in love with you too."

At that moment, I realized I simply didn't have the heart to continue fighting for a marriage where my wife didn't share the same vision of a partnership I had. I informed Donna I was done when I returned home.

We finalized our divorce in 2012. It wasn't easy for either of us. At the tender age of seven, our daughter Olivia was grappling with the aftermath of a harrowing hospital stay, which had subjected her to a seemingly endless series of procedures and surgeries. In the wake of these medical challenges, she now faced the additional upheaval of our divorce. I was steadfast in my resolve to shield her from the brunt of this transition, determined to ensure that the changes in our family dynamic would not diminish her sense of security and love.

I wanted more than anything for Olivia to understand, deep in her heart, that despite the shifts in our family structure, our love for her remained unwavering and unconditional. It was crucial for me that she emerge from this period of change with her spirit intact, knowing she was cherished beyond measure by both of her parents.

It was a complicated few months. Donna is a good woman and a great mother to our daughter. She ultimately married a great guy, Rod, whom I highly respect and admire. He has been an awesome stepdad to my daughter, and he treated her like his own in the time she spent at their home. Donna and Rod have been together ever since, they married in 2013, and they have a great partnership.

Cambria, too, was in the midst of a divorce. She had two daughters who were seven and nine, and my daughter was also seven.

We had a million things to work out. We opted to put our heads together and create a plan for a life together. To do so, we had to separate ourselves from dozens of people who wished to change our minds.

We had to ensure that how we acted for ourselves and for our daughters would be in everyone's best interests.

We applied our skills as performance coaches and created a plan that would best serve our daughters, families, and careers.

Eventually, Cambria and I married in the summer of 2015, the same year we opened our first real estate brokerage, Haven Real Estate Group in Spokane, Washington.

Since then, Cambria and I have become friends with Donna and Rod. We made them dinner on our dock at the lake for a recent anniversary. To emphasize how connected we are, we recently became investors in Rod's start-up company, and we're thrilled with what he is building. They are frequent visitors to our home as we are in theirs.

When Cambria and I became a couple, I suddenly found myself transitioning from being a dad to one, to a father of three wonderful girls. Each one added their distinct character and demands to the mix, transforming my life into a colorful mosaic filled with both trials and delights. Reflecting back, I can confidently say that embracing this role has been the most transformative journey of my life.

I was determined to give them the best of me, to be the dad they truly deserved. There's something incredibly special about having daughters. They have this unique ability to bring out the best in you, to make you strive to be a better man. It's a gift unlike any other.

Men and women experience and process the world differently. With a partner, it's easy to dismiss these differences and not fully understand their perspective. But with my little girls, I couldn't just let it be. Their hearts were my responsibility. I constantly asked them to help me understand their feelings and share their world with me.

I dove into books on fatherhood, specifically on being a dad to daughters. I wanted to be exactly what they needed. My goal was not just to be a supportive dad, but to nurture their independence, instilling in them values and principles to guide them through life.

Together with Cambria, we introduced them to Personal Development courses like "The Landmark Forum" and Tony Robbins' "Unleash the Power Within." These experiences taught them to face their fears head-on, even if it meant walking barefoot across hot coals. The idea was simple yet profound: conquer your fears here, and you can tackle any challenge life throws at you.

I remember Jordan Peterson, a Canadian psychologist, emphasizing the importance of the ages between four and twelve as the prime time to shape and influence your children. In my experience, he was spot on. As our daughters stepped into their teenage years, their world expanded, and their friends, their friends' parents, and their teachers began to play a bigger role in their lives.

This journey of fatherhood has been a roller coaster of emotions and learning experiences, and I wouldn't have it any other way.

Madison, or Mady as we affectionately call her, is our youngest and was just seven years old when I first became a part of her life. Winning her trust and affection took time, over four years. She was always polite and respectful toward me, but I could tell she was guarding her heart, secretly hoping for her mom and dad to reunite.

Determined to build a strong connection with each of my girls, I made a point to spend quality one-on-one time with them. I'd surprise them with lunch at school or run errands together, just the two of us.

During one of our outings, as Mady shared stories about her dad, I felt compelled to reassure her. "Honey, I'm not here to take your dad's place. He will always be your father. I don't want you to feel like you have to choose between us. When I married your mom, I committed to being here for you, to being a dad to you. And I love every moment of it. It's an honor to be a part of your life." That conversation marked a turning point for us, and over the years, our bond has only grown stronger.

Mady is a whirlwind of curiosity and adventure. Our talks often revolve around her latest learnings and observations, showcasing her deep passion for knowledge. At sixteen, she became a certified scuba diver, and she's my go-to dive buddy, always calm, confident, and in control under the sea. She's just as comfortable in a paintball arena as she is during a spa day, a blend of interests she shares with her sisters.

Standing out in her high school class of over 2,000, Mady graduated with an associate's degree, one of only six students to do so. Her insatiable thirst for knowledge even led her to explore psychology, prompting hours of deep conversations and analysis of life patterns.

The summer before college, Mady took her sense of adventure and compassion to the Philippines for seven weeks of volunteer work, fully funded by her own savings. While we missed her terribly and worried about her being so far from home, we couldn't help but feel immense pride. She returned from her journey transformed, radiating a newfound confidence and maturity.

Now eighteen, Mady is in Canada, pursuing her bachelor's degree, and while our home feels emptier without her, our hearts swell with pride. Each time she visits, our first priority is to plan her next return, ensuring that as she heads back to college, we're already counting down the days until we're reunited.

Olivia, or Livie as we affectionately call her, is my daughter from my previous marriage to Donna. At just seven years old, only a few months older than Mady, she found the transition to our new family setup quite challenging.

From being an only child, she suddenly had two sisters and seemed to perceive them as rivals for my attention and love. Adding to the complexity, her mother played the role of a nurturer and friend, while I maintained a more disciplined environment at our home. This led Livie to prefer staying with her mother, which was initially tough for me to handle.

A counselor underscored the importance of sticking to our principles, assuring me that Livie would eventually understand and appreciate them. Being the enforcer of rules was exhausting, especially with Livie's defiant nature at that time. Her life experiences, from health struggles in the hospital to her parents' divorce and suddenly gaining siblings, turned her into a precocious child, constantly challenging and testing boundaries. It felt like a never-ending cycle for Cambria and me, making progress over the weekend only to start from scratch the next.

Initially, Livie harbored resentment toward Cambria. To ease the tension, Cambria would run errands when I brought Livie home because her presence seemed to trigger Livie's attitude. This small adjustment helped reduce the friction between them.

Counseling played a vital role once again, teaching me to respond to Livie's defiance with a calm, factual connection between her choices and their consequences, and to clearly communicate our expectations. I believed that with consistent love and unbiased reinforcement of consequences, Livie would eventually learn to navigate life's rules successfully.

A heartbreaking moment came when Livie, at eighteen and still in high school, decided to move out, wanting to live life on her terms. With limited funds, an unreliable car, and her education hanging by a thread, I feared she was heading down a difficult path. Her words, comparing her choices to my and Cambria's past mistakes, hit me hard. I worried our relationship might be at risk and that she'd be too proud to seek our help.

Contrary to my fears, Livie maintained her connection with our family. She celebrated her freedom, perhaps a bit too exuberantly for my liking, but she managed to graduate, joined our family dinners, and regularly invited me to lunch. Cambria's advice to step back and offer friendship rather than advice proved invaluable. As I embraced this approach, Livie and I grew closer, and one day, she expressed her desire to come back home.

Now back under our roof, Livie is serious about her future, pursuing a career in nursing. It's a joy having her home, and she's truly grateful for the support we provide. We've always aimed to uplift our daughters, and it's heartwarming to see Livie finally embracing that and expressing her gratitude.

Kiaya, our eldest daughter, was ten when I entered her life. We instantly formed a unique bond. She has a different father than her sister Mady, but that never mattered; we just clicked. Kiaya sensed my dedication to being the best possible dad and naturally gravitated toward me. Of all her sisters, she's the most sensitive, feeling the highs and lows of life more intensely, with her emotions quickly bubbling to the surface.

I soon realized that Kiaya needed ample nurturing and encouragement. She shone in grade school, constantly seeking her teachers' approval and setting high standards for herself. This desire for perfection carried on into middle school, where the challenge of pleasing multiple teachers added to her sensitivity. When she started taking an interest in boys, she struggled to balance her desire to please everyone.

A moment that fills me with immense pride is when, at thirteen, she asked me to adopt her. I was utterly speechless. What an incredible honor—she wanted me to be her dad. Her heartfelt words conveyed her deep appreciation for my love and care, highlighting how I always put the children first. She made it clear: she wanted me to be her official dad.

I'll never forget the day in the courtroom when my brave thirteen-year-old girl confidently told the judge she wanted me to become her legal father. The room fell silent as the judge asked a series of questions, ensuring this was genuinely her wish.

When it was my turn to speak, all I could say was, "Your honor, I can't even imagine a world where I wouldn't want to be her dad."

We've navigated the turbulent waters of her teenage years together, learning and growing along the way. She'll always hold a special place in my heart, and I am eternally grateful she chose me as her dad.

Recently, she joined our firm as a real estate agent, giving me the wonderful opportunity to mentor her as she builds her career.

Truly, my daughters are the greatest blessings in my life.

## The Journey to Becoming Entrepreneurs

Not long after Cambria and I became a couple, we embarked on the venture of establishing a real estate team. Cambria swiftly showcased her innate ability to connect with prospective homeowners, seamlessly guiding them through the intricate journey of home-buying.

Our synergy was undeniable, and it wasn't long before we tapped into the leadership skills honed through various development courses. We envisioned a team where we could mentor new agents, equipping them with the necessary tools to carve out successful careers in real estate.

Just as we were gaining momentum, an unexpected twist unfolded. The manager of our brokerage, a franchise of one of the nation's real estate giants, summoned me to his office, delivering the startling news: They were letting me go.

During my tenure with the company, I had ascended from a greenhorn agent to a mentor, often leading classes on marketing and lead generation. I had even earned a spot on the brokerage's version of a board of directors. My affinity for the company was profound; they championed a mission, vision, and values that resonated deeply with my own beliefs. However, I found myself at odds with them in private meetings, particularly when discussions revolved around decisions impacting my fellow agents. I couldn't help but challenge them, pointing out inconsistencies and urging for actions that truly reflected the values they professed. "Are these values that we proudly display just a catchy marketing strategy, or do they genuinely hold meaning?" I had once passionately implored the brokerage owner and its managers.

Looking back, I recognize my naivety regarding the underlying politics. My candor, although well-intentioned, was not well-received. So, when Cambria and I were abruptly dismissed, it was a bitter pill to swallow, albeit not entirely unforeseen. Fortunately, it didn't take us long to find refuge in another firm, securing a new professional home within a day.

That unceremonious exit planted the seeds for a dream: to establish our own brokerage, steadfastly adhering to values we held dear, irrespective of convenience. This resolve was further solidified when our previous firm withheld commissions rightfully owed to us, amounting to thousands of dollars. We envisioned a brokerage grounded in integrity, honesty, and professionalism—a sanctuary for agents to learn, grow, and provide unparalleled service to our clients.

Fast forward to today, and our dream has come to fruition. Our firm is lauded as the top real estate agency in the region according to consumer ratings. While we may not be the largest, our focus isn't on size. Our priority is cultivating an environment where our agents feel at home, empowering them to build enduring relationships and a career that supports their aspirations.

For Cambria and me, this journey has been immensely fulfilling. Our reputation among consumers is a source of pride, and the opportunity to play a pivotal role in our agents' success is both an honor and a privilege.

Despite our success, we are not without detractors. Competitors occasionally attempt to tarnish our reputation, whispering to potential recruits, "Did you know one of the owners is a former bank robber?" Rather than taking offense, we welcome these comments with gratitude. Little do our critics realize that their attempts to undermine us inadvertently become our greatest recruitment tool. Our agents consistently outperform industry averages, and those who transition from other firms often see their sales double. Our success and positive reviews speak volumes, piquing the interest of agents even more when they hear these rumors.

I once harbored anxieties about my past coming to light, fearful of judgment and misconceptions. Yet, I've discovered that authenticity and transparency have the power to resonate with people on a deeper level. Many agents have expressed that working with someone who openly acknowledges their mistakes and has surmounted numerous challenges is refreshing and inspiring.

Do the naysayers deter some? Absolutely. But I've come to accept that I'm not everyone's cup of tea—and that's perfectly okay. There is a profound liberation in looking in the mirror, recognizing your flaws, and still striving to be the best version of yourself. Whether as a husband, father, friend, neighbor, employer, coach, or entrepreneur, I stand tall, knowing I give my all in every facet of life. For those who may not see my worth, I sincerely hope they too find their peace and contentment in life.

Together, Cambria and I have navigated many storms, including the intricacies of raising teenage girls, while also carving out time to build our own relationship with each other. Together, we've built businesses that did a billion dollars a year in home sales while also enjoying a life of travel and fun together.

The lesson I most wish to share about overcoming adversity is that adversity is going to happen. In today's digitally dominated world, social media can paint a misleading picture of unblemished lives, leading many to live under the illusion of perpetual perfection. However, it's imperative to acknowledge that life is inevitably filled with highs and lows. The lows are certain and unavoidable, and the real key to a fulfilling life lies in acquiring the skills to effectively navigate through these challenging times. Many live blissfully unaware, almost oblivious to the inevitable challenges life will present, underscoring the crucial importance of being prepared and equipped to face and overcome life's inevitable obstacles.

Mike Tyson famously said, "Everyone has a plan until they get punched in the mouth."

## Self-Reflection

Taking the time to answer the questions below thoughtfully will be pivotal in fostering true growth and transformation. These questions are crafted to challenge your thought patterns and reactions, arming you with tools to approach adversity with resilience and integrity. Reflecting on and documenting your responses will provide invaluable insights, equipping you to navigate challenges in the future with newfound strength and clarity. Your progress lies in understanding and applying these understandings to your personal journey.

## Questions to Reflect On

1. How have you experienced the delicate balance between personal and professional relationships, and how might an accountability coach support you in navigating them?

2. Considering your own adversity, how can the principles of accountability and commitment be applied to overcome your challenges?

3. How have your reactions to unexpected changes, similar to my realization of my feelings for Cambria, shaped the trajectory of your personal journey?

4. Reflecting on Mike Tyson's quote about everyone having a plan until they get punched in the face (face a setback), how has unforeseen adversity changed your plans?

5. When facing adversity, how have you sought out support or accountability, and how might formalizing that support, as I did with Cambria, change the outcomes?

6. How do the principles of integrity and commitment outlined in this chapter resonate with your personal experiences, and how can you harness these principles to shape your responses to future challenges?

**Summary**

- **Acknowledge Your Feelings:** Recognize and accept your emotions during setbacks. Understanding your feelings allows you to navigate your path forward with greater clarity and authenticity.

- **Seek Accountability:** Partner with someone you trust, or consider getting an accountability coach. When you have someone to share your goals with, you're more likely to remain committed to achieving them, even in the face of adversity.

- **Set Clear Goals:** Define your personal and professional objectives. By knowing what you're working toward, you can better align your actions and decisions, especially during challenging times.

- **Develop Resilience:** Remember that setbacks are a natural part of any journey. By building resilience, you'll be better prepared to face adversity head-on and bounce back more robustly.
- **Continuously Reflect and Adjust:** Regularly evaluate your path and adapt as needed as you progress. Understanding plans might need to change when faced with adversity ensures you remain flexible and can pivot accordingly.
- **Prioritize Integrity:** Ensure you're acting with integrity in all decisions and actions. When you act authentically and with a strong moral compass, overcoming adversity becomes a challenge you face with honor, making the journey more fulfilling.

## Conclusion

Life is a mix of challenges and triumphs, and overcoming adversity is a skill you can hone and master. Embracing accountability and building genuine connections can lead to personal and professional growth. It's a lesson in the importance of commitment even when faced with unexpected twists and turns.

Think of your life as a road. You will face obstacles, detours, and unexpected stops, but you can navigate any situation with the right mindset.

As you move forward, use these insights as tools. Lean into accountability, value the relationships you build, and remember challenges can be steppingstones to greater things. It's not just about avoiding obstacles but learning from them and coming out stronger on the other side.

Embrace challenges with determination, foster genuine connections, and remember that every experience, good or bad, contributes to your growth. With the right mindset and tools, you're well-equipped to tackle anything life throws at you.

# UNLEASHING YOUR OWN POTENTIAL

with Robert Henry

# 11

# SELF-LEADERSHIP: CHARTING YOUR PERSONAL PATH TO SUCCESS

*"Success isn't a destination; it's a continual process of learning, adapting, and evolving."*

— Malcolm Gladwell

Reflect for a moment on the most impactful leaders or bosses in your life—the ones for whom you were willing to give your absolute best. These exceptional individuals have a unique way of creating a nurturing environment, ensuring that those under their guidance feel acknowledged, secure, confident, and shielded. This kind of leadership elevates individual performance and strengthens the collective bond of a team, setting the stage for both personal and shared success.

Now, let's dive a bit deeper. Think of a time when you felt truly seen by a leader, when they took the time to connect with you, recognize your efforts, and empathize with your challenges. This cultivated a sense of belonging and motivation to give your best. In environments where you felt safe, trust and consistent support were abundant, encouraging you to share your ideas and take risks without fear of judgment. Feeling accepted meant your unique qualities and contributions were valued, leading to a genuine and productive engagement. And when you felt protected, it was because you knew you had a leader who had your back, ready to navigate challenges together.

These are the hallmarks of great leadership. But what if I told you that the most crucial leader in your life is, in fact, you?

In this chapter, "Self-Leadership: Charting Your Personal Path to Success," we will explore the journey from external reliance to internal empowerment. My own path, which took a drastic turn within the confines of a federal prison, is a testament to the transformative power of self-leadership. From a troubled past and a life of crime, I made a resolute decision to change the trajectory of my life, investing in my personal growth, education, and development.

Imagine treating yourself with the same level of respect, empathy, and support that you would expect from the best leaders in your life. It starts with internalizing the feelings of being seen, safe, accepted, and protected.

Consider my friend Adam, a bodybuilder passionate about health and fitness. Adam has a personal standard that embodies the essence of self-leadership. He allows himself the grace to miss a day at the gym, but never two in a row. This approach integrates leniency with determination, ensuring a single setback doesn't spiral into defeat. It's a structured way of replacing self-criticism with constructive action.

Feeling seen in the context of self-leadership translates to self-awareness, recognizing your efforts, and understanding your emotions. Feeling safe means cultivating an inner sanctuary of compassion and forgiveness. Acceptance at this level is about embracing your true self, imperfections, and all, while feeling protected involves being your own advocate and setting healthy boundaries.

As we delve into this chapter, I invite you to embark on a journey of self-discovery and empowerment, learning to lead yourself with the same care, respect, and dedication the best leaders provide. Self-leadership is like navigating a ship through the vast expanse of the open sea. The captain within you takes charge, steering through calm waters and turbulent storms with equal resolve, guided by an internal compass calibrated by your values, beliefs, and vision for your life.

### Navigating the Depths: Defining Self-Leadership

Self-leadership is the art of leading oneself, akin to being the captain of your own ship. It involves understanding your thoughts, emotions, and behaviors and taking proactive steps to guide them in a direction that aligns with your aspirations and values. It is a dance between introspection and action, between awareness and decisiveness.

### Key Components of Self-Leadership:

- **Self-Awareness:** Like a lighthouse guiding ships in the night, self-awareness illuminates your internal world, helping you understand your strengths, weaknesses, emotions, and reactions.

- **Self-Regulation:** This is your ability to control or redirect disruptive impulses and moods and the discipline to think before acting. The steady hand on the wheel maintains course despite the waves.

- **Self-Motivation:** Propelling your ship forward, self-motivation is the wind in your sails, driving you toward your goals with passion and perseverance.
- **Self-Reflection:** This is your compass, a tool for regular introspection, ensuring your actions align with your values. It will lead you to course corrections when necessary.
- **Self-Empowerment:** Empowering yourself is like hoisting the sails high, embracing the power within to face challenges and seize opportunities.

### The Currents of Influence: External Leadership and Self-Leadership

While self-leadership focuses on leading oneself, external leadership involves being led by others. Think of external leadership as the currents and winds that affect your ship. They can guide you, push you forward, or present challenges. The most profound leaders are like favorable winds, lifting you up and propelling you forward. However, the true test of self-leadership is how you navigate when the winds are not in your favor.

### The Four Anchors of Self-Leadership:

1. **Being Seen:** In self-leadership, being seen is akin to recognizing your own reflection in the water. It is acknowledging your worth, efforts, and journey, and appreciating the ripples you create in the vast sea of life.

2. **Being Safe:** Providing yourself a safe harbor is about creating a mental space where you are free to express your thoughts and emotions, take risks, and learn from mistakes without the crushing weight of self-judgment.

3. **Being Accepted:** Like a ship finding its place in the harbor, being accepted is about embracing who you are, quirks, and all. It acknowledges that even the most seasoned ships have scars and barnacles, and that's perfectly okay.

4. **Being Protected:** To be protected in self-leadership is to have your own back to support your values and well-being. It's the fortified lighthouse, standing tall and unwavering, ensuring you stay true to your course.

In navigating the self-leadership journey, you become the captain, the navigator, and the ship, moving with purpose through the seas of life. By cultivating self-awareness, self-regulation, motivation, reflection, and empowerment, and anchoring yourself in feelings of being seen, safe, accepted, and protected, you chart your own course toward a life of fulfillment and success.

### Embarking on the Journey Within: The Role of Self-Awareness in Self-Leadership

Navigating the landscape of self-leadership is akin to setting sail on a personal voyage of discovery, where the winds of self-awareness fill your sails and guide you toward uncharted territories of personal growth and enlightenment. Just as a seasoned sailor understands the importance of being attuned to the subtle whispers of the wind and the rhythmic patterns of the sea, an effective self-leader recognizes the pivotal role of self-awareness in steering the course of their life.

### The Illuminating Power of Self-Awareness

Self-awareness is like a bright star guiding you through the night, helping you see your journey of leading yourself with clear eyes and understanding. It's all about looking inside yourself, paying attention to your thoughts, feelings, and actions, and being really open and curious about what you find. Think of it as a mirror showing you who you really are, helping you dig deep to understand what drives you, what scares you, and what you truly want.

Take my own life as an example. In moments when I find myself getting frustrated with my wife and on the verge of snapping at her, I stop and reflect. I remind myself of the promises I made to her on our wedding day—to love, respect, honor, and cherish her, no matter what. I didn't say, "I'll do all these things unless I've had a tough day." So, even when conflicts come up, I work hard to make sure my actions reflect those vows. I won't lie and say I'm perfect at it, but I do catch myself before I say or do something that goes against my standards and my promises to her. And if I ever do slip up, I'm quick to apologize. This approach really helps to keep trust strong in our marriage, which is crucial.

When you work on being more self-aware, you're giving yourself the tools to get through life's challenges with strength and poise. You become more in tune with your own values and goals, and you know when you need to correct your course to stay true to them. Building this self-awareness is the first step to transforming yourself and finding your own path to success and happiness.

## Cultivating a Garden of Growth: Adopting a Growth Mindset

Imagine your mind as a fertile garden, teeming with potential and ripe for cultivation. Adopting a growth mindset is like tending to this garden, nurturing the seeds of possibility and embracing the challenges and obstacles that arise as opportunities for growth and learning. It is a belief in the malleability of your abilities and the power of effort, a conviction that with dedication and perseverance, you can cultivate the skills and qualities needed to thrive.

When you embrace a growth mindset, you transform challenges into steppingstones, viewing failures not as insurmountable roadblocks, but as valuable feedback on your journey of self-discovery. You become a resilient gardener, undeterred by the weeds of doubt and the pests of criticism, steadfast in your commitment to nurture your garden to its fullest potential.

## The Symphony of Emotional Intelligence: Harmonizing Emotions and Actions

Picture yourself as the conductor of a grand symphony, where your emotions are the musicians, each playing their unique instrument in your life's orchestra. Emotional intelligence is the mastery of conducting this symphony, harmonizing your emotions and actions to create a symphony of self-leadership.

Emotional intelligence involves the ability to recognize and understand your own emotions, as well as the emotions of others, and to use this awareness to manage your behavior and relationships effectively. Like a skilled conductor, you learn to listen attentively to the melodies of your emotions, discerning their nuances and appreciating their significance in the broader composition of your life.

With emotional intelligence, you navigate the highs and lows of your emotional landscape with grace and poise, transforming dissonance into harmony and uncertainty into confidence. You become adept at managing stress, empathizing with others, and resolving conflicts. You cultivate a balanced and resilient mindset that propels you on your self-leadership journey.

### Charting the Course Ahead

As you navigate the voyage of self-leadership, let the winds of self-awareness fill your sails, guiding you toward a life of purpose and fulfillment. Embrace the growth mindset as your compass, viewing challenges as opportunities for learning and transformation. Conduct your symphony of emotions with grace and poise, harmonizing your inner world to create a masterpiece of self-leadership. In doing so, you become the master of your own destiny, charting your course with clarity, insight, and unwavering determination.

### Cultivating a Nurturing Inner Environment

Embarking on a self-leadership journey is akin to nurturing a garden within ourselves. Just as a garden requires fertile soil, adequate sunlight, and regular care, our inner world needs a nurturing and supportive environment to flourish. However, at times, weeds of self-deception may sprout, clouding our self-perception and hindering our growth.

Self-deception acts as a fog, blurring the lines between reality and perception. It convinces us to wear a mask, hiding our true selves and areas of growth. We may tell ourselves stories that justify our actions, even when they don't align with our values or the leader we aspire to be. It's like looking in a distorted mirror, seeing only what we want to see and remaining blind to the parts of ourselves that need attention and care.

The key to overcoming this self-deception is vulnerability, a courageous act of peeling back the layers and facing our true selves, warts and all. It's about having the bravery to acknowledge our imperfections, our fears, and our mistakes. Like a gardener tending to a garden, we must be willing to pull out the weeds of self-deception, making room for authenticity and growth.

Creating a nurturing inner environment requires self-compassion and a non-judgmental attitude. It's about treating ourselves with the same kindness and understanding we would offer a close friend. When we make a mistake or face a setback, instead of beating ourselves up, we can offer ourselves grace and encouragement to try again.

## Strategies for Creating a Nurturing and Supportive Internal Environment

Strategies to cultivate this supportive inner world include practicing mindfulness, which helps us stay grounded and centered in the present moment. Journaling can also be a powerful tool, providing a space for self-reflection and gaining insights into our thoughts and behaviors. Additionally, establishing a network of supportive relationships provides us with a safety net, reminding us that we are not alone in our journey.

In essence, the journey of self-leadership is an ongoing process of tending to our inner garden, ensuring it has all it needs to thrive. By overcoming self-deception through vulnerability, practicing self-compassion, and creating a nurturing and supportive inner environment, we pave the way for personal growth and transformation, ultimately becoming the leaders of our own lives.

### The Power of Self-Compassion and Acceptance

When navigating the labyrinth of life, it's easy to become our own harshest critic, often forgetting the power of self-compassion and acceptance. Imagine a sapling striving to grow in a harsh environment. The more it is exposed to harsh conditions without support, the harder it becomes for it to flourish. Similarly, our inner selves require nurturing and care to develop into the best versions of ourselves.

Stephen R. Covey, in his book *The 7 Habits of Highly Effective People*, introduced the principle of proactivity, emphasizing the significance of taking responsibility for our own lives. Proactivity is like the gardener deciding to water and tend to the sapling, regardless of the external conditions. It is about understanding that we have the power to shape our responses to life's challenges. Coupled with a personal vision, which serves as a compass directing us toward our true north, we find a powerful duo for fostering self-compassion.

Just as a sapling has its unique blueprint for growth, each of us is driven by intrinsic motivation, a concept brought to light by Daniel H. Pink in his book *Drive*. Understanding and tapping into our intrinsic motivation means recognizing our innate needs for autonomy, mastery, and purpose. It's like the sapling recognizing its need for sunlight, water, and nutrients. When we align our actions with our internal drives, we cultivate a sense of self-acceptance and personal fulfillment.

So, how can one nurture self-compassion and acceptance in daily life? Here are some practical examples and exercises:

- **Journaling:** Take a few moments each day to reflect on your actions, thoughts, and feelings. Write down three things you did well and one thing you could improve on. Rather than criticizing yourself for the improvement area, approach it with curiosity and kindness, exploring ways to grow.

- **Positive Affirmations:** Create a list of positive affirmations that resonate with you. Repeat them daily, especially during challenging times. Remember that, like the sapling, you are a work in progress, deserving of care and compassion.

- **Mindfulness and Meditation:** Engage in mindfulness practices or meditation, focusing on being present and accepting of your current state. This practice can be visualized as giving the sapling the space to breathe and grow, free from the constraints of weeds or shadows.

- **Gratitude Practice:** At the end of each day, list three things you are grateful for. This helps shift the focus from what went wrong to appreciating life's small wins and positive aspects.

By integrating these practices into your daily routine, you actively nurture your inner sapling, providing it with the compassion and acceptance it needs to grow and thrive. Remember, the journey to self-leadership is a continuous process, and just like a garden, it requires regular care and attention. Embrace the power of self-compassion and acceptance, and watch as you flower into the leader you are meant to be.

## Setting and Achieving Personal Standards

Embarking on a journey of self-leadership is akin to navigating a ship through uncharted waters. To successfully guide your vessel, it's imperative to clearly understand your personal *why*, the beacon of light that gives meaning and direction to your journey.

Understanding your personal *why* is like uncovering the compass hidden within you, one that points toward your true north. It illuminates the path to setting meaningful and fulfilling goals, ensuring that each step you take is aligned with your core values and purpose. Just as a captain charts a course based on a desired destination, you, too, can chart your course through life with intention and clarity.

Once your *why* is crystal clear, the next step in your voyage is setting your sails toward your goals, employing the concept of SMART goals as your navigational tools. SMART, an acronym for Specific, Measurable, Achievable, Relevant, and Time-bound, ensures your goals are well-defined and attainable. Setting SMART goals is like plotting specific coordinates on your map, providing a clear and structured path to reach your destination.

However, setting the course is only part of the journey. Upholding personal standards serves as the wind in your sails, propelling you forward with consistency and integrity. Personal standards are your commitments to yourself, the unwavering principles guiding your actions and decisions. They are the codes of conduct you uphold, regardless of the weather or the challenges that arise.

Embracing these principles and setting and achieving personal standards becomes a transformative form of self-leadership. It is about taking the helm and leading yourself with conviction and accountability. Just as a captain leads their crew with confidence and integrity, you can lead yourself through the highs and lows of your journey.

Take, for instance, the captain who navigates through a storm, upholding their standards of courage and resilience, guiding their ship to safety. Similarly, when faced with adversity, your personal standards serve as your anchor, grounding you in your values and guiding you to make choices that align with your *why*.

In essence, setting and achieving personal standards is the rhythm of the dance between knowing your *why* and navigating toward it with precision and authenticity. It is about aligning your actions with your values, steering your ship with purpose, and leading yourself to the shores of fulfillment and success.

## Building Resilience and Accountability

Embarking on the path of self-leadership is like setting out to climb a mountain. It requires a strong foundation of personal resilience and a steadfast commitment to reaching the summit, regardless of the challenges that may arise.

Building personal resilience is a crucial aspect of self-leadership. It's about cultivating an inner strength that allows you to bounce back from setbacks, learn from failures, and keep moving forward. Like a tree that bends in the wind but doesn't break, resilience provides the flexibility and toughness needed to navigate life's storms.

Delve into the transformative insights from Jim Collins' book *Good to Great* and adapt these powerful strategies for your personal growth and self-leadership journey. This process is akin to unlocking a wellspring of wisdom, propelling your development to unprecedented heights. This journey transcends merely recognizing your strengths; it demands a fervent commitment to excellence and embedding profound discipline in every facet of your life.

Reflect on the world's most successful companies: They meticulously select the right individuals and strategically position them to thrive. Similarly, effective self-leadership necessitates the cultivation of a supportive inner circle, individuals who resonate with your values and are courageous enough to hold you accountable when you deviate from your path.

Here are some strategies to help you build accountability and resilience in your journey of self-leadership:

- **Embrace Challenges:** View challenges as opportunities for growth. Each obstacle is a steppingstone, leading you closer to your goals.

- **Reflect and Learn:** After each setback, take time to reflect. What can you learn from this experience? How can you use these insights to move forward?

- **Set Clear and Achievable Goals:** Establish clear and realistic goals. Break them down into manageable steps and celebrate your progress.

- **Foster a Supportive Network:** Surround yourself with people who encourage and challenge you. A strong support network is like a safety net, catching you when you fall and helping you to bounce back.

- **Practice Self-Compassion:** Be kind to yourself, especially in moments of failure or doubt. Remember that growth often happens in the face of adversity.

- **Maintain a Growth Mindset:** Cultivate a mindset that embraces challenges and is open to learning. Remember, resilience is not a fixed trait but a muscle that can be strengthened over time.

- **Take Responsibility:** Own your actions and their outcomes. Taking responsibility empowers you to make changes and move forward.

Self-leadership is a journey of building personal resilience and accountability. It's about navigating through life's challenges with strength and grace, steering your ship with purpose, and holding yourself accountable to reach the summit of your potential. So, embrace the climb, stay resilient, and be the captain of your journey, leading yourself toward greatness.

### Creating a Legacy of Self-Leadership

Self-leadership is not just a tool for personal development; it's a canvas upon which the masterpiece of your life is painted. The strokes you make, the colors you choose, and the images you create all contribute to the legacy you leave behind. Your legacy is not just what you leave for people; it's what you leave in them.

Think of your life as a garden. Self-leadership is diligently tending to this garden, ensuring your planted seeds grow into strong, resilient trees. The fruits of these trees are the impact you have on the world, the sweet nectar of a life well-lived. Your garden, lush and vibrant, becomes a source of inspiration and nourishment for others long after you are gone.

Imagine you are an author and your life is a book. Each chapter represents a phase of your life filled with highs and lows, triumphs and tribulations. Self-leadership is your ability to write your story with the intention of choosing the narrative that aligns with your values and aspirations. It's about being the hero of your story, not a passive character swept along by the tides of circumstance.

Your legacy is the book you leave behind, a timeless tale that continues to inspire and guide future generations. It's the wisdom in the pages, the courage in the characters, and the strength in the story. Through self-leadership, you ensure your book is worth reading, a story that echoes through the ages.

Encourage your readers to ponder: What story am I writing with my life? What seeds am I planting in my garden? Through self-leadership, they have the power to craft a legacy that is meaningful, impactful, and a beacon of inspiration for others to follow.

Nelson Mandela's life epitomizes a journey of extraordinary self-leadership, transforming personal hardship into a legacy of freedom and equality.

Born in apartheid-era South Africa, Mandela could have succumbed to bitterness and anger. Instead, he chose a path of resilience and forgiveness. He spent twenty-seven years in prison, maintaining his dignity and commitment to his cause, even in the face of brutal conditions.

Upon his release, Mandela didn't seek vengeance. He pursued reconciliation and unity, leading South Africa out of the dark apartheid era and into a new age of democracy. As the country's first Black president, he worked tirelessly to dismantle systemic racism and foster a spirit of inclusivity.

Mandela's legacy is a testament to the power of self-leadership. He turned personal suffering into a source of strength, leading by example and showing the world that forgiveness is more powerful than hatred and that unity can triumph over division.

In his own words, "As I have said, the first thing is to be honest with yourself. You can never have an impact on society if you have not changed yourself.... Great peacemakers are all people of integrity, of honesty, but humility."

Mandela's life reminds us that self-leadership is not just about guiding ourselves; it's about inspiring and uplifting others. He showed us that we can create a legacy that shapes a better world for generations to come with resilience, forgiveness, and a steadfast commitment to our values.

In the end, the journey of self-leadership is a journey of legacy, a journey of creating a life that shines brightly and lights the way for others. Embrace this journey, live with intention and purpose, and leave behind a legacy of strength, wisdom, and love.

## Self-Reflection

As we reach the end of this chapter, let's take a moment to reflect on the journey we've traversed, exploring the nuances and transformative power of self-leadership.

We began by defining self-leadership as the art of leading oneself toward achieving one's potential, focusing on nurturing feelings of being seen, safe, accepted, and protected. We recognized that self-leadership isn't just a solo journey; it's influenced by external leadership but requires inner strength and direction.

We then dove into the world of self-awareness, acknowledging its pivotal role in self-leadership. Like a compass in a sailor's hand, it guides us through the stormy seas of life, ensuring we stay true to our course. We talked about the growth mindset and emotional intelligence as the sails of our ship, helping us navigate various challenges with grace and resilience.

Cultivating a nurturing inner environment was our next port of call, understanding that self-deception can cloud our journey. At the same time, vulnerability acts as the sunshine, dispelling the fog and allowing us to see our path clearly.

We embraced self-compassion and acceptance as our anchors, ensuring that we stay grounded and secure in times of turmoil. We acknowledged that our internal dialogue should be as a kind and encouraging mentor, not a harsh critic.

Setting and achieving personal standards was our map, guiding us toward our true north. Understanding our personal *why* and aligning our actions with our goals ensure that our journey is meaningful and fulfilling.

Building resilience and accountability was our ship's sturdy hull, protecting us from the crashing waves of adversity and keeping us afloat even in the toughest storms.

Finally, we discussed creating a legacy of self-leadership, understanding that the journey doesn't end with us; it ripples outwards, influencing others and leaving a lasting impact on the world.

Self-leadership is the journey of a lifetime. It's about taking the helm of our ship, navigating through calm and stormy seas, and steering toward a life filled with purpose, impact, and fulfillment. It requires self-awareness, resilience, and a deep commitment to our values and goals.

As you turn the pages of this book and continue on your journey, remember that you are the captain of your ship. The power to lead yourself toward success and fulfillment lies within you. Take the helm, set your course, and sail toward your horizon. The journey of self-leadership awaits.

As you reach the culmination of this chapter, I invite you to pause and engage in a deep, reflective exercise that transcends the surface level of understanding.

Below are meticulously crafted questions to provoke thought, challenge existing patterns, and pave the way for transformative change in your life, especially in adversity. Remember, the true essence and progress from the material you've absorbed lie in the authenticity and depth with which you answer these questions. They are keys to unlocking new perspectives, tools, and strategies to fortify your integrity and resilience. Don't just skim the surface; dive deep, explore uncharted territories within yourself, and emerge with newfound wisdom and strength. This is your moment to translate learning into actionable insight to bridge the gap between knowledge and practice. So, take a deep breath, embrace vulnerability, and let the journey of self-reflection begin.

**Questions to Reflect On**

1. Reflect on a recent challenge you faced. What patterns of thought or behavior did you notice, and how did they impact the outcome?

2. In moments of adversity, what role does your internal dialogue play, and how can you transform it into a more supportive and empowering voice?

3. How does your current support network influence your resilience and accountability, and in what ways can you strengthen these connections?

4. Consider a time when you faced a setback. How did you respond, and what could you have done differently to foster growth and learning?

5. What personal standards do you hold yourself to, and how do they align with your values and goals? Are there any adjustments needed to ensure congruency?

6. Reflect on the legacy you wish to create through self-leadership. What steps can you take today to start building towards that legacy?

7. How does your understanding of self-leadership influence the way you navigate challenges, and what shifts in perspective or behavior are necessary for your growth journey?

**Summary**

- **Cultivate Self-Awareness:** Develop a deep understanding of your values, beliefs, and behaviors. Regular self-reflection helps you identify areas for growth and understand your reactions to different situations, ensuring you stay true to your path.

- **Embrace a Growth Mindset:** Adopt a mindset that sees challenges as opportunities for development. Cultivate resilience by learning from failures and setbacks, and understand that your abilities can be developed with effort and perseverance.

- **Build a Supportive Inner Circle:** Surround yourself with individuals who share your values and are not afraid to provide constructive feedback. A strong network acts as a sounding board and provides support in times of need, enhancing your self-leadership journey.

- **Set and Achieve Personal Standards:** Define clear and achievable goals that align with your values and aspirations. Break these goals into actionable steps, celebrate your progress, and adjust your course when necessary to stay on track.

- **Practice Self-Compassion and Acceptance:** Treat yourself with kindness, especially in moments of failure or doubt. Acknowledge your emotions without judgment, and remember that setbacks are integral to the growth journey.
- **Leave a Lasting Legacy:** Reflect on the impact you want to have on the world and take intentional steps to create a positive legacy. Live purposefully, share your wisdom, and inspire others through your self-leadership journey.

**Conclusion**

As we wrap up our journey on self-leadership, let's pause to take stock of what we've learned and how far we've come. This journey has been about finding your strength, understanding yourself better, and standing firm when faced with challenges.

You've learned to navigate tough times, using self-awareness as your guide and resilience as your shield. You've realized the importance of having a support system and being kind to yourself, especially when things don't go as planned.

Your journey doesn't end here. The skills and knowledge you've gained are tools that will serve you well in the future. Remember, it's about making consistent choices that align with your values and goals and not being afraid to take the lead in your own life.

You are now better equipped to handle whatever comes your way. Keep pushing forward, learning, and leading yourself with confidence and integrity. Your self-leadership journey is unique, and it's all about making your path and following it with determination.

So, keep your head high and your steps steady. You've got this!

# UNLEASHING YOUR OWN POTENTIAL

with Robert Henry

# 12

# EMBRACING A BEGINNER'S MIND: THE POWER OF CURIOSITY AND CONTINUOUS LEARNING

*"Life's greatest challenge is not to conquer the world but to constantly rediscover it. Each day presents a new lesson, a new opportunity to learn and grow."*

— Friedrich Nietzsche

Imagine stepping back in time to when you were a toddler with wide eyes full of wonder and limitless imagination. In that world, even something as simple as a paperclip was more than just a tool for holding papers together—it was a treasure chest of endless possibilities. Perhaps it was a dragon's wing, a mini sword for a toy knight, or a crown for your teddy bear. In the eyes of a child, imagination knows no bounds.

This isn't just sentimental nostalgia; it's the premise of an eye-opening study conducted by Sir Ken Robinson, an esteemed authority in education and human potential. Robinson carried out an experiment delving into the depths of creativity and the human mind involving

1,500 toddlers. The task was straightforward, yet the implications were profound: What all can you do with a paperclip?

The findings were astonishing. A staggering 98 percent of these toddlers found more than 200 unique uses for that single paperclip. Their minds transformed it into objects adults could scarcely fathom—illustrating how we are all, essentially, born to be creators, thinkers, and dreamers. The fabric of our very existence seems woven with an inherent ability to innovate.

However, as time marched on, the study revealed something unsettling. The boundless landscape of these young imaginations began to narrow. By age seven or eight, only 30 percent could muster the same level of creativity they had displayed as toddlers. As they moved into their teens, that number shrank to a mere 12 percent. By the time they were eighteen and standing at the threshold of adulthood, just 3 percent retained the limitless imagination that once defined them.

What could account for this drastic decline? Was it the rigid structure of formal education? The societal pressure to conform? Robinson's study pried open a Pandora's box of questions that challenge our understanding of creativity, learning, and the trajectory of human potential itself.

So, what's the takeaway for us? Well, it appears that we begin our journey through life as vibrant canvases, brimming with the colors of curiosity and wonder. But as we navigate the complexities of life, these colors tend to fade, as if sculpted by invisible hands. This is more than mere metaphor; it's a cautionary tale about the self-imposed cages we can find ourselves in. Without a commitment to lifelong learning, we run the risk of narrowing our worlds and limiting our ability to recognize opportunities when they come our way.

The question that looms before us is this: How do we escape becoming one of the 97 percent who lose that critical creative edge? The answer may not lie solely in keeping our creative juices flowing, but rather in adopting a broader perspective—lifelong learning.

Lifelong learning goes beyond acquiring a new skill or hobby. It's an enduring mindset, a steadfast commitment to the idea that our brains are always capable of growth and transformation, regardless of age. It's the realization that every moment is a classroom, every experience a lesson. Whether you're immersed in a captivating novel, watching the sun dip below the horizon, sharing a laugh with a loved one, or even listening to the simple rhythm of a heartbeat, there is something to learn.

So, in the end, Sir Ken Robinson's groundbreaking study serves as more than just a testament to the importance of nurturing creativity; it's a rallying cry for a culture of continuous learning. It emphasizes that intellectual growth is not bound by age, and that the realms of knowledge and creativity stretch far beyond the walls of any classroom or the pages of any curriculum. It's a compelling reminder that, no matter where we are in our life's journey, we should strive to keep our minds free and our eyes open to the endless possibilities that surround us.

This chapter serves as more than just an exposition. It's a journey, an exploration of the realms of what we can become when we allow ourselves to remain students of life. The age-old adage rings true: The more we know, the more we realize how little we know.

## Discovering the Spark of the Beginner's Mind

Have you ever felt that itch to rediscover the world through fresh eyes? That's what we're diving into today: the magic of the Beginner's Mind. Think of it as seeing things without all the baggage, as if it's your first time, every time. And believe me, it's a game-changer.

Remember when you were a kid? Every day was an adventure. The smallest things—a butterfly, a puddle, even a cardboard box—could be a universe of possibilities. That child, that curious explorer, still lives inside you. And that's the secret sauce we're tapping into.

Now, don't get me wrong. The Beginner's Mind isn't about tossing out all you know or pretending you're five again. It's about blending our life's experiences with the spark and curiosity we all started with. It's about looking at everyday challenges and saying, "Okay, what can I learn here?" instead of, "Not this again."

Imagine you're at a dance party. The Beginner's Mind isn't about having the best moves; it's about enjoying the music, laughing when you miss a beat, and getting right back into the groove. It's that simple joy of dancing like no one's watching.

Life, with all its twists and turns, is your dance floor. And the Beginner's Mind? It's your favorite dance partner—the one who whispers, "Let's try a new move!" It encourages you to step out of your comfort zone, to ask questions, to laugh at mistakes, and to celebrate every little win.

Think of the Beginner's Mind as your all-access pass to life's vast library. Every book, every page, holds something new. And your burning *why*—your purpose and passion—is the flashlight helping you find the most thrilling reads.

In the world of personal growth, staying curious and open is the real secret sauce. With the Beginner's Mind in your toolkit, you're not just going through the motions. You're actively engaging, growing, and lighting up from the inside. Challenges? They're puzzles waiting to be solved. Setbacks? Just plot twists in your personal epic.

## The Transformative Power of Curiosity

Imagine being a kid again. You're in your backyard and you see a butterfly. It's not just an insect; it's a mysterious creature that seems to dance in the air. Remember how a simple cardboard box could transform into a spaceship, or a castle, or a racecar? That same sense of wonder is what I'm talking about—unfiltered curiosity. And guess what? That wide-eyed explorer is still you—it's just that life's been busy handing you scripts to read from, dulling that innate sparkle.

The Beginner's Mind isn't about forgetting everything you've learned or pretending you're back in kindergarten. Nah, that's not it. It's about blending the wisdom of your years with your original zest for life. Instead of groaning, "Oh, no, not this again," when faced with a challenge, you're saying, "All right, life, what's the lesson today?"

So, let's visualize this: You're at a dance party—yes, even if you're the type who avoids the dance floor like it's hot lava. The Beginner's Mind doesn't care if you have zero dance moves or a whole arsenal. It's about feeling the beat, messing up, laughing it off, and jumping right back into it. It's not about dancing to impress; it's about dancing to express.

Picture life as that dance floor. You're there, not just swaying awkwardly on the sidelines but tearing it up with joy, even when life throws you a curveball. Your Beginner's Mind is like the infectious friend who gets everyone dancing, the one who whispers, "Hey, let's try that ridiculous move!" when a new song comes on. This is the attitude that propels you out of your comfort zone, urging you to ask questions, learn from missteps, and celebrate the small victories like they're standing ovations.

Now, think of the Beginner's Mind as a VIP pass to the world's most magnificent library. You're not just browsing; you're on a treasure hunt. Each book, each page offers a new opportunity to learn something thrilling. And that burning question you have, your *why*—your life's passion and purpose—is like a flashlight that highlights the most riveting chapters tailored just for you.

You see, in the quest for personal growth, being eternally curious is your ace in the hole. When you hold onto your Beginner's Mind, you're not sleepwalking through life. You're wide awake, soaking up experiences like a sponge in a puddle. Challenges become exciting puzzles screaming to be solved. And setbacks? They're just juicy plot twists in the incredible story of *you*.

## The Odyssey of Lifelong Learning

By now, you've journeyed with me through the darkest corridors and brightest clearings of my life. In my story, I've shared the ins and outs of my tumultuous past: from a childhood where love and understanding were often foreign languages to the twisted corridors of criminal life. And if I've learned anything from those life lessons, it's this—learning never stops. Not even behind bars. So, let's dig into what I like to call "The Odyssey of Lifelong Learning," shall we?

First off, let me be crystal clear: I'm not referring to the paint-by-numbers, standardized-test kind of learning you've endured in the classroom. Forget that straight-jacket approach. Instead, let's talk about learning as an audacious, wind-in-your-hair journey across an ocean so endless you can't see where it starts or ends. Each wave you ride, each challenge you overcome, is a new chapter in your life's story. You're not just bobbing up and down, trying to keep your head above water—you're conquering new territories, hungry for what lies beyond the next horizon.

Picture yourself not as a mere tag-along, but as the captain of your own fate. You know that incessant, nagging voice inside that constantly asks "Why?" or "How?"—that's your internal compass. It's your gut telling you there's more to see, more to discover. And you know what? Your life experiences, your unique perspective, that's your vessel—custom-built and unlike any other, it's designed to navigate the labyrinth of the known and unknown.

Yet even the most exhilarating quests have their ordeals. Just like Odysseus had to face storms and sea monsters, you too will encounter your share of trials. Picture waves towering like skyscrapers, threatening to throw you off course. But here's where we flip the script—these aren't setbacks or disasters; they're your rites of passage. These trials forge you, honing your skills, shaping your resilience, and priming you for the bigger, more awe-inspiring challenges that lie ahead.

All right, let's tackle the elephant in the room—the overwhelming deluge of information we face today. In this era, where a smartphone can offer more knowledge than ancient libraries, it's all too easy to feel like you're drowning. How do you set your course in this whirlpool? The answer is your *why*, your guiding light.

Your *why* is your life's mission statement. It's the glue that holds your journey together when the going gets tough. It sifts through the noise and distraction, illuminating the gems that resonate with you most. You see, your *why* isn't just a beacon, it's your sanctuary in the storms of life. With it, you can turn the hurricane of the digital world into a propellant, pushing you toward your destination faster.

So no, lifelong learning isn't just another to-do list item to tick off and forget. It's your lifeline, your gateway to a world teeming with wonders you can't yet imagine. Every day gives you another chance to unfurl those sails, jump back into that boundless ocean of knowledge, and discover new territories within and around you.

Here's the sum of it all: Your life is an odyssey, and you're the hero and the narrator. Your insatiable curiosity is your compass, the unique lens of your experiences is your ship, and your deeply rooted *why* is your anchor. When you stitch all these elements together, what you get is a grand adventure, an epic saga with endless chapters yet to be written. So, what are you waiting for? Set sail and chart your course into the thrilling seas of lifelong learning. Trust me, those horizons won't discover themselves.

## Cultivating a Beginner's Mind

Now, let's talk about a cornerstone that has turned my life around:

the cultivation of a Beginner's Mind, that evergreen sense of awe and wonder that drives the pursuit of lifelong learning. And let's be clear—rekindling that fire within you will take some work, but boy, is it worth it!

First off, let's pause to take stock of that tiny spark deep within you—that's your curiosity. It's like an ember nestled in the ashes of a long-extinguished fire, just waiting for the right gust of wind to spring back to life. Now, to turn that ember into a roaring blaze, you've got to humble yourself a bit. You've got to look yourself in the mirror and say, "Hey, I don't know everything, and that's totally cool." In fact, it's liberating.

Think of curiosity as your personal guide through the wild, untamed forests of knowledge. Sure, some paths are well-trodden and easy to navigate, but the real gems? They're off the beaten path, where you've got to hack your way through overgrown foliage and navigate around natural obstacles. Every swat of your machete, every step into the dense underbrush, propels you farther into the realm of your untapped potential.

Let's get real: Curiosity takes a solid dose of courage. Imagine standing on the edge of a cliff, peering into the dark abyss below, and thinking, *What if jumping is the key to soaring?* I won't sugarcoat it—the risks are there, but so is the incredible thrill of discovery. The magic lies in shifting your perspective, seeing each obstacle not as a roadblock but as a steppingstone launching you toward greater understanding.

But what about setbacks? Ah, setbacks. They're your unsolicited travel companions on this journey. Do you know how mountain climbers face treacherous terrain, sudden storms, and occasional setbacks, yet press on? They dig their heels in, not because the climb gets any easier, but because their resolve hardens into something impenetrable. That's what you call grit—the raw, unyielding determination that turns every challenge into a rousing cry of "Bring it on!"

I get it—sometimes learning feels like trying to complete a million-piece jigsaw puzzle. The sheer scope of what you don't know can be overwhelming. But instead of staring at the giant blank space, focus on fitting together the pieces you do have. And if that nagging voice of self-doubt starts whispering in your ear, let your newfound resilience be the booming rebuttal. Each time life throws you a curveball, remind yourself, "This isn't a step backward; it's setting the stage for an epic comeback."

Here's the grand finale: Lifelong learning isn't a sprint—it's a marathon. Forget about some imaginary finish line where you suddenly know "enough." There's no such thing. It's about the relentless journey, the insatiable quest to grow, expand, and transform. Remember that study by Sir Ken Abraham about the declining creativity in children as they move through the educational system? Don't let the system do that to you. Keep the awe, keep the wonder, and cultivate a Beginner's Mind.

## Conclusion

As we reach the closing lines of this odyssey, I'm overwhelmed with a deep sense of gratitude. Thank you for taking this journey with me, for walking through both the shadows and the light of my life's story. Your willingness to accompany me on this rollercoaster of ups and downs humbles me, and I truly hope my experiences serve as both a mirror and a window for you—a mirror reflecting your own potential and a window revealing vistas of possibilities you might not have considered before.

I'm not going to pull any punches here. The path to your dreams isn't going to be a stroll in the park. You will stumble and face setbacks that might seem insurmountable. Yet, here's the beautiful paradox—each setback carries within it the seeds of resilience, strength, and wisdom. With every challenge you conquer, you become not only more robust but also more nuanced as a person. And believe me, the bigger the obstacle, the more lavish the rewards on the other side.

Take setbacks as your life's curriculum, tailor-made for you. They are not obstacles but steppingstones, each one laying the foundation for your indomitable spirit. Each is a lesson, a gift, an opportunity for growth. As you amass these gifts, you'll find that future setbacks seem less like towering walls and more like hurdles—challenging, sure, but far from insurmountable.

And let's be crystal clear: The world is in dire need of leaders—people willing to step up, take action, and blaze new trails. We need leaders who not only dream but also do. That leader could be you. Yes, you, reading these very words. Whether your sphere of influence is a household, a community, or an entire corporation, you have the power to make waves of change.

So, I urge you, as you close this book, don't let the story end here. Take these words, these lessons, and use them as fuel for your own magnificent journey. Build the life of your wildest dreams, brick by brick, choice by choice. You owe it to yourself and the world to unfurl those sails, raise that anchor, and navigate toward horizons only you dare to explore.

From the bottom of my heart, thank you for letting me be a small yet heartfelt part of your grand expedition. Your own thrilling saga awaits—go write it, live it, be it. And always remember, each new day brings with it the promise of a fresh start and a new adventure.

With utmost gratitude and endless encouragement,

Robert Henry

# UNLEASHING YOUR OWN POTENTIAL

*with Robert Henry*

# RECOMMENDED READING

**Mindset & Self-Belief:** These books will help you understand the power of positive thinking, resilience, and self-confidence. Developing a growth mindset can serve as the cornerstone for personal and professional success.

- *Mindset: The New Psychology of Success* by Carol S. Dweck
- *The Power of Now: A Guide to Spiritual Enlightenment* by Eckhart Tolle
- *Think and Grow Rich* by Napoleon Hill
- *You Are a Badass: How to Stop Doubting Your Greatness and Start Living an Awesome Life* by Jen Sincero
- *Atomic Habits: An Easy & Proven Way to Build Good Habits & Break Bad Ones* by James Clear

**Personal Development:** Investing in personal development is akin to planting seeds in fertile soil and consistently nurturing them until they blossom into sturdy trees. Personal development is a lifelong commitment to becoming the best version of yourself, and it's pivotal for several reasons if you want to lead a life that's not just successful but also happy and fulfilled. These books will help.

- *The 7 Habits of Highly Effective People* by Stephen R. Covey
- *How to Win Friends and Influence People* by Dale Carnegie
- *The Power of Now* by Eckhart Tolle
- *Daring Greatly* by Brené Brown
- *The Subtle Art of Not Giving a F*ck* by Mark Manson
- *Atomic Habits* by James Clear
- *Drive: The Surprising Truth About What Motivates Us* by Daniel H. Pink

**Emotional Intelligence:** With these books, you'll learn better how to manage and express emotions effectively, and develop empathy and understanding for others' feelings. Emotional intelligence is an underrated skill that can improve both personal and professional relationships.

- *Emotional Intelligence* by Daniel Goleman
- *Social Intelligence* by Daniel Goleman
- *Working with Emotional Intelligence* by Daniel Goleman
- *Primal Leadership* by Daniel Goleman, Richard Boyatzis, and Annie McKee
- *Emotional Intelligence 2.0* by Travis Bradberry and Jean Greaves

**Personal Relationships & Social Skills:** Whether it's friendships or family bonds, relationships form a critical part of overall happiness. With these books, you will learn how to foster deep, meaningful connections and improve social intelligence.

- *How to Win Friends and Influence People* by Dale Carnegie
- *Influence: The Psychology of Persuasion* by Robert B. Cialdini
- *The 5 Love Languages* by Gary Chapman
- *Men Are from Mars, Women Are from Venus* by John Gray
- *Crucial Conversations* by Al Switzler, Joseph Grenny, and Ron McMillan

**Romantic Relationships & Marriage:** These books will help you focus on the essential qualities of a fulfilling romantic relationship and how to keep the marital spark alive. Communication, trust, and mutual respect are key.

- *Hold Me Tight* by Dr. Sue Johnson
- *The Seven Principles for Making Marriage Work* by John Gottman
- *Attached: The New Science of Adult Attachment and How It Can Help You Find—and Keep—Love* by Amir Levine and Rachel Heller

- *Passionate Marriage* by David Schnarch
- *The Relationship Cure* by John Gottman and Joan DeClaire
- *Why Marriages Succeed or Fail* by John Gottman
- *Love Sense* by Dr. Sue Johnson

**Career & Professional Development:** These books offer tips for achieving success in the workplace, from essential soft skills to strategies for climbing the corporate ladder or thriving as an entrepreneur.

- *What Color Is Your Parachute?* by Richard N. Bolles
- *Deep Work: Rules for Focused Success in a Distracted World* by Cal Newport
- *Thinking, Fast and Slow* by Daniel Kahneman
- *Crucial Conversations* by Al Switzler, Joseph Grenny, and Ron McMillan
- *StrengthsFinder 2.0* by Tom Rath

**Time Management & Productivity:** These books teach methods to make the most out of a twenty-four-hour day, promoting work-life balance and avoiding burnout.

- *Getting Things Done* by David Allen

- *Eat That Frog!* by Brian Tracy
- *The 4-Hour Workweek* by Timothy Ferriss
- *Essentialism: The Disciplined Pursuit of Less* by Greg McKeown
- *The Power of Habit* by Charles Duhigg
- *Make Time: How to Focus on What Matters Every Day* by Jake Knapp and John Zeratsky

**Overcoming Obstacles & Resilience:** These books provide the tools to tackle challenges head-on, learn from failures, and turn setbacks into comebacks.

- *Man's Search for Meaning* by Viktor E. Frankl
- *Grit: The Power of Passion and Perseverance* by Angela Duckworth
- *The Obstacle Is the Way* by Ryan Holiday
- *You Are a Badass* by Jen Sincero
- *The Resilience Factor* by Karen Reivich and Andrew Shatté
- *Make Your Bed: Little Things That Can Change Your Life...And Maybe the World* by Admiral William H. McRaven
- *The Gifts of Imperfection* by Brené Brown

- *Unbroken: A World War II Story of Survival, Resilience, and Redemption* by Laura Hillenbrand

**Financial Literacy & Wealth Building:** Understanding budgeting, saving, investing, and debt management can provide not just financial freedom but also peace of mind. These books will teach you what you need to know.

- *Rich Dad Poor Dad* by Robert Kiyosaki
- *The Millionaire Next Door* by Thomas J. Stanley and William D. Danko
- *The Intelligent Investor* by Benjamin Graham
- *The Richest Man in Babylon* by George S. Clason
- *Your Money or Your Life* by Vicki Robin and Joe Dominguez
- *I Will Teach You To Be Rich* by Ramit Sethi
- *The 4-Hour Workweek* by Timothy Ferriss
- *The Little Book of Common Sense Investing* by John C. Bogle

**Physical Health & Wellness:** These books emphasize the importance of a balanced diet, regular exercise, and adequate sleep. Good physical health often translates into improved mental well-being.

- *How Not to Die* by Michael Greger
- *The China Study* by T. Colin Campbell and Thomas M. Campbell II
- *Eat, Move, Sleep* by Tom Rath
- *The Blue Zones* by Dan Buettner
- *Why We Sleep* by Matthew Walker

**Purpose & Legacy:** These books encourage readers to contemplate what they want to be remembered for and how they can make a meaningful difference in the world or their community.

- *Start with Why* by Simon Sinek
- *The Alchemist* by Paulo Coelho
- *Legacy* by James Kerr
- *The Hero with a Thousand Faces* by Joseph Campbell
- *The War of Art* by Steven Pressfield
- *Outliers: The Story of Success* by Malcolm Gladwell
- *Your Best Year Ever* by Michael Hyatt
- *How Will You Measure Your Life?* by Clayton Christensen

- *The Road Less Traveled* by M. Scott Peck
- *Finding Your Element* by Sir Ken Robinson
- *What Matters Most* by Hyrum W. Smith
- *Flow: The Psychology of Optimal Experience* by Mihaly Csikszentmihalyi
- *Essentialism: The Disciplined Pursuit of Less* by Greg McKeown

# UNLEASHING YOUR OWN POTENTIAL

*with Robert Henry*

# ABOUT THE AUTHOR

Robert Henry's life story, intricately detailed in *Unleashing Your Own Potential: The Self-Leadership Journey from Rock Bottom to Prosperity and Beyond*, is a profound journey from adversity to triumph. Robert's early life, marred by crime and poor choices, dramatically changed course during his five-year sentence in federal prison. This became a pivotal time for introspection and education, as he consumed more than 700 books, completed his high school education, and took numerous college courses, setting the foundation for his transformation.

Now more than twenty years since his release, Robert has invested more than a million dollars in his own growth, exploring fields like psychology, leadership, and performance coaching. This journey has transformed him into a sought-after keynote speaker and performance coach, as well as a thriving real estate entrepreneur, co-founding businesses like Haven Real Estate Group and Haven Mortgage. He's developed unique training programs that have made a real difference for real estate agents, loan officers, and those he coaches, helping them unlock their potential and achieve success.

In his book, Robert shares not just his journey, but the practical strategies and lessons that have shaped his path to prosperity. He challenges readers to embark on their own self-leadership journeys, armed with resilience and determination.

Now living a balanced life in the Pacific Northwest with his wife and business partner, Cambria, and their three daughters, Robert is a testament to the power of change and the potential within everyone to achieve greatness. His story is not just inspiring; it's a call to action for anyone ready to take control of their life and journey toward fulfillment and success. Don't miss the chance to learn from his experiences and unleash your own potential.

# UNLEASHING YOUR OWN POTENTIAL

with Robert Henry

# BOOK ROBERT HENRY TO SPEAK AT YOUR NEXT EVENT

Bring a speaker to your next event who has experienced the darkest lows and the highest highs of life. Introducing Robert Henry—a man whose life journey from a challenging childhood, a past in bank robbery, and time spent in prison, to investing over a million dollars in personal transformation, embodies resilience and self-belief.

**Why Choose Robert Henry for Your Event?**

- **A Story Unlike Any Other:** Robert's journey is unique, filled with challenges and transformative lessons that captivate and inspire.
- **Personal Leadership Focus:** While others may speak on team dynamics or organizational leadership, Robert zeroes in on self-leadership, sharing tools and insights for personal growth and success.
- **Captivating Engagement:** Whether speaking to a small group or a large audience, Robert's real-life stories and actionable strategies create a deep, meaningful connection.
- **A Mix of Humor, Passion, and Wisdom:** Expect sessions that are not just informative, but also emotionally stirring, filled with humor and passion, designed to motivate and encourage action.

Transform your event into an unforgettable experience with Robert Henry. Explore his most impactful moments and check his availability on his website: www.UnleashingYourOwnPotential.com/book-robert.

Contact Robert for a no-obligation pre-event chat, and rest assured that Robert's speaking fee is all-inclusive, covering travel, accommodation, and other expenses. No hidden costs or surprises.

Save more with Robert's Pre-Pay Option, and inquire about volume discounts on his book, *Unleashing Your Own Potential*, a perfect gift for attendees that ensures the inspiration continues long after the event.

Don't miss out on the chance to work with a top-tier speaker. Engagements fill up quickly, so contact Robert Henry today to secure your spot and make your next event truly exceptional.

**(509) 413-9634**

**Robert@HavenRealEstateGroup.com**

**www.UnleashingYourOwnPotential.com**

# UNLEASHING YOUR OWN POTENTIAL

With Robert Henry

# ROBERT HENRY COACHING

If you're ready to elevate your life and unlock your fullest potential, Robert Henry is the coach you've been searching for. With a background as captivating as his coaching methods, Robert's life has been a roller coaster from a troubled past to a triumphant present, making him uniquely equipped to guide you through your personal and professional journey.

**Transform Your Life with Real-Life Wisdom:** Robert's own transformation is nothing short of extraordinary. He has navigated through life's darkest moments and emerged stronger and wiser. As your coach, he shares this hard-earned wisdom, providing practical tools and strategies grounded in real-world experience to help you craft the life you desire.

**Commitment to Your Growth:** Robert has invested more than a million dollars in mastering the art of personal development. His extensive knowledge in psychology, leadership, and performance coaching ensures that you're getting top-tier, comprehensive guidance. He's not just a coach; he's a relentless advocate for your potential.

**Tailored Strategies for Lasting Change:** Robert's approach goes beyond surface-level solutions, aiming for deep, lasting transformation. He works with you to identify and overcome obstacles, creating a personalized roadmap to success and fulfillment. With Robert, it's not just about short-term gains; it's about building a foundation for lifelong achievement.

**Support and Challenge:** Robert knows when to offer a compassionate ear and when to challenge you to reach new heights. He's committed to helping you hold yourself accountable, ensuring that you stay on track and remain resilient in the face of adversity.

**Leverage Real-World Expertise:** With a successful career in real estate and entrepreneurship, Robert offers invaluable insights for those aspiring to excel in business. His coaching is enriched with practical lessons from the field, giving you an edge in your entrepreneurial endeavors.

Take the leap and partner with a coach who offers more than just advice—a coach who offers a partnership in your journey to success. Visit https://unleashingyourownpotential.com/coaching/ and start transforming your life with Robert Henry today. Don't just dream of a better life; make it a reality. Contact Robert today.

**(509) 413-9634**

**Robert@HavenRealEstateGroup.com**

**www.UnleashingYourOwnPotential.com**